The
MYSTERY
of

B
JE

The
MYSTERY
of
BEING
JEWISH

Molly Cone

UAHC Press

New York, New York

Library of Congress Cataloging-in-Publication Data

Cone, Molly.
  The mystery of being Jewish.

  Bibliography: p.
  Summary: Presents biographies of men and women
whose Jewishness influenced their lives and whose
lives often had an extraordinary influence on the
world around them.
  1. Jews—Biography—Juvenile literature.
[1. Jews—Biography] I. Title.
DS115.C62 1989   920'.0092924 [B] [920] 88–29631
ISBN 0–8074–0401–2

To my children and grandchildren

Acknowledgments

Writing this book not only filled every spare moment in my life for many months but encroached on the lives of my family and many of my friends, whose interest in the idea of this book encouraged me as I went along. Not only am I grateful to them but also to my husband, Jerry, for his patience in listening, copyreading, and being cheerfully helpful whenever I needed advice.

I particularly owe much to my editor, Aron Hirt-Manheimer, who met my suggestion for this book with interest and enthusiasm and as much personal cooperation as any writer could wish for from an editor. My thanks, too, to Joy Weinberg, editor of *Reform Judaism*, for unfailing cooperation whenever I needed it.

Special thanks to Jeanette Schrieber and members of her Chavurah group; to Kay Crane, librarian; to Dr. Arthur Lagawier, Dr. Belle Ruth Witkin, Rabbi Norman Hirsch, and Rabbi Vicki Hollander. Special thanks, too, to my grandson, Joshua Dale, whose able research saved me countless hours; and to fellow writers of *Rejects* for their critical eye and unabating interest.

Contents

About This Book

Not all who read this book will agree with what's in it. Some may shake their heads, even frown, at the thoughts expressed here or at the particular personalities I selected to demonstrate these thoughts.

That is perfectly all right. Among Jews, diversity is considered a very good thing. Differing opinions are so natural in most Jewish lives that there are many age-old jokes about it.

One I like goes something like this:

A rabbi, after listening to the complaint of one neighbor against another, says, "You are right." After listening carefully to the second neighbor, the rabbi nods and also says, "You are right."

"But," said his wife, "they can't both be right." Thoughtfully, the rabbi considers his wife's words. "You know," he said finally, "you are right, too."

That is typical of a Jewish joke, but it's also typical of a certain kind of wisdom that came out of centuries of study of the Torah. In the Talmud, one of the most revered books of the Jews, differing opinions fill the margins around the main text on every page. In houses of study, throughout the ages, the air above those pages was thick with argument. Jews are used to disagreement. Discussion and debate have traditionally been a part of their lives.

Since Israel became a state, there has been more and more discussion about "Who is a Jew?" and "What is a Jew?" Those are not easy questions to answer. Great minds have offered answers and equally great minds have disagreed with those answers. In the words of a scholar: "Question, investigation, dispute, dissent—these are bone and flesh of the tradition."

This book began with a question—a question that started me off, unwittingly, into looking for clues to the mystery of being Jewish. It was an adventure of discovery. Did I follow a golden brick road stretching invitingly out toward a castle on a hill? No. The trail I took was more like going from crumb to crumb through a thick forest with no end in sight.

This book is a summary of my odyssey. Its pages are filled

with accounts of some of the people I encountered along the way. They are an important part of this book because only through them and others like them did I finally perceive what had been mostly hidden from me: the strengths of Jewishness.

In this book you will read about men and women whose Jewishness influenced their lives and whose lives had a strong and good, often extraordinary, influence on the greater world around them.

It was pointed out to me that presenting individuals from this viewpoint could appear to be chauvinistic. Some said that it might be looked upon as a claim of Jewish superiority. (They pointed to scoundrels, racists, and villains—who were also Jews.)

They were right, of course. That was possible. But it's also possible that, like the rabbi's wife in the Jewish joke, I am right, too.

The process of writing this book was a little like the process used by restorers of valuable old paintings. They scrape off years of soot and dirt and retouchings until they get down pretty close to the original paint. In writing this book, I scraped down far enough to see clearly my Jewish self.

Perhaps this book will help others to do the same.

"Properly, the Jew ought hardly to be heard of. . . ."

If the statistics are right, the Jews constitute but one-quarter of one percent of the human race. . . . Properly, the Jew ought hardly to be heard of, but he is heard of, has always been heard of. . . . His contributions to the world's list of great names in literature, science, art, music, finance, medicine, and abstruse learning are very out of proportion to the weakness of his numbers.

> Mark Twain
> *Harper's* magazine
> September 1897

A **Maimonides,** in the twelfth century, was one of the greatest minds of the Middle Ages. A **Spinoza,** in the seventeenth century, was one of the greatest modern philosophers. A **Freud** gave to the twentieth-century world a whole new approach to people's emotions and their problems. And an **Einstein** opened a new understanding of the world of energy and matter, thus of the entire physical universe.

Everyone in the world today, Raphael Patai pointed out in his book *The Jewish Mind* (1977), is affected in one way or another by the products of the minds of those men and of other Jews of great accomplishment.

The theory of relativity, the science of psychoanalysis, cybernetics, holography, modern neurophysiology, bacteriology, chemotherapy, Salvarsan for the treatment of syphilis, and the polio vaccine were all discovered or developed by Jews. So were vitamins, dietetics, logical semantics, method acting, the atomic submarine, the hydrogen bomb, and the "Big Bang" theory of the creation of the universe.

Half the Jews in the world today live in the United States. Their number? Three percent of the population of this country. Yet they have won 27 percent of the Nobel Prizes awarded American scientists.

Jews are overrepresented in medicine by 231 percent in proportion to the general population, reported the authors of *Why the Jews?* (1983), in psychiatry by 478 percent, in dentistry by 299 percent, and in mathematics by 238 percent.

That so few could contribute so much has been a puzzlement to more than one observer of history. Through the ages, it has remained a mystery.

1
THE MYSTERY OF BEING JEWISH

(One view) Israeli artist Yaacov Agam's *Star of Love*.

*There are depths to
Jewishness which even
rabbis and scholars
cannot fathom.*

Sigmund Freud, founder of psychoanalysis, was seventy years
old when he wrote in a letter: "Only to my Jewish nature did I
owe the two qualities which had become indispensable to me on
my hard road."

Because he was a Jew, he said, his mind was free to question
all things. And, *being a Jew*, he was used to standing his ground
in the face of all opposition.

What was Freud talking about? What did he mean by "Jewish"
nature?

According to the dictionary, your "nature" is the combination
of qualities that make you what you are.

Was a Jewish nature different from other kinds? I wondered.
If so, how was it different? And that's how I began what became
a yearlong quest of discovery.

What was I looking for exactly? I didn't know. But looking I
began to find it. And what I found began to form into patterns,
and the patterns began to repeat themselves.

"There are unconscious depths to the phenomenon of Jewishness
which even those of us who have spent our lives in its study
cannot fathom," wrote Richard Rubenstein, a rabbi and scholar.

This belief was expressed again and again, in one way or another,
in books of Jewish history and philosophy and biography. It appeared frequently in articles and stories and essays.

With a growing sense of excitement, I searched through book
after book.

"It is something inside the individual that makes him a Jew,"
said the philosopher and theologian Franz Rosenzweig. He called
it "something infinitesimally small yet immeasurably large."

Perhaps, more than many, he knew what he was talking about.
Brought up as an assimilated Jew, Rosenzweig, at one time, decided
to convert to Christianity. He changed his mind on a fateful Yom
Kippur eve—when that something within him caused him to re-
claim his Jewishness.

That mysterious "something" present in the Jewish makeup was

3

noted by others who lived long before Rosenzweig. In the Yiddish language, it was called *"dos pintele Yid." Yid* is the Yiddish word for "Jew"; *pintele* is the Yiddish word for "dot," originally meaning the tiny point that stood for the letter *yud* of the Hebrew alphabet.

Dos pintele Yid translates into "the dot of a Jew" and was used to mean the quintessence of one's Jewish identity. According to a Yiddish legend, told to me by an elderly Jewish scholar: "Even though the *dot* may be no greater than half the size of a pomengranate seed, it has the capability to bloom within the self and from it may come—who knows?"

Again and again, throughout the 4,000 years of the history of the Jews, the truth of the legend of the dot proved itself.

No other writer of history has recorded the experiences of the Jews as passionately as has Will Durant, a non-Jew, in his book, *The Story of Philosophy* (1938). He presented 2,000 years of Jewish history in one breathless sentence:

> Driven from their natural home by the Roman capture of Jerusalem (70 A.D.), and scattered by flight and trade among all the nations and to all the continents; persecuted and decimated by the adherents of the great religions—Christianity and Mohammedanism—which had been born of their scriptures and their memories; barred by the feudal system from owning land, and by the guilds from taking part in industry; shut up within congested ghettos and narrowing pursuits, mobbed by the people and robbed by the kings; building with their finance and trade the towns and cities indispensable to civilization; outcast and excommunicated, insulted and injured;—yet, without any political structure, without any legal compulsion to social unity, without even a common language, this wonderful people has maintained itself in body and soul, has preserved its racial and cultural integrity, has guarded with jealous love its oldest rituals and traditions, has patiently and resolutely awaited the day of its deliverance, and has emerged greater in number than ever before, renowned in every field for the contributions of its geniuses, and triumphantly restored, after two thousand years of wandering, to its ancient and unforgotten home.

A sociologist once asked a distinguished philosopher, a Jew driven from Germany by the Nazis, his definition of a Jew. "A man who feels a stranger everywhere," he replied.

"Strangers everywhere" is almost two thousand years of Jewish history in two words. Yet, even though they were separated by the passing of generations and lived scattered over the world, never were they strangers to each other.

No matter how far Jews may be removed from their origins, their faith, or their people, most cannot help feeling a sense of elation when a Jew is honored. And, when one of their number is found guilty of misdoing, most other Jews feel tarnished by it. This strong bond of kinship was wrapped tightly around the Jewish nation even during those centuries when there was no nation.

Elie Wiesel in his book, *One Generation After* (1970), tells a story of a young Jew in King Herod's time, who took a favorite pillow with him when he left Jerusalem to travel to Rome. One night, the pillow burst into flames. The Temple in Jerusalem was destroyed by fire that night and the Jewish nation with it.

To be Jewish, said Elie Wiesel, is to live a thousand miles away from the Temple and see it burning.

Most Jews today still wake with a flaming pillow when something occurs that affects the Jewish people.

"We Jews are a community based on memory," wrote the philosopher and scholar Martin Buber, in 1932. "Sons and grandsons have the memory of their fathers and forebears in their bones." (And daughters and granddaughters in theirs.)

The memory he was talking about was not the one you use when you think about your trip to Disneyland. It was not the same memory you use for your friends' telephone numbers and your favorite jokes and the tunes of the songs you like to sing. Buber was not talking about your usual kind of memory.

Rather, he meant the kind of memory that goes back into history to the people you came from. He meant the kind of memory that gives you shoulders to stand on—that helps you to see beyond your own personal view.

Some call this kind of memory "a community of memory." Buber called it a "collective memory."

A Jew's collective memory goes all the way back to Abraham. Gathered through centuries, it comes from the whole of Jewish tradition and Jewish experience. It is every Jew's inheritance.

Speaking to today's young Jews, Elie Wiesel said:

> You have seen Moses at Sinai—heard David in his citadel—
> fought the Romans at Masada—felt the crusader's sword
> . . . died at Auschwitz—Your *I* includes them all.

Every Jew is 4,000 years old—I heard those strange words many times before I discovered what they really meant. They originally came from Leo Baeck. He, like Elie Wiesel, was talking about the collective memory.

Recorded in a Jew's collective memory are not the times and places of the momentous events in Jewish history. Stored there, instead, are the essential *attitudes* that came out of living the events.

For example, Jewish people today don't know much about the years their ancestors lived as slaves in Egypt. What they know, instead, is that they *love freedom* and *hate oppression*. They hate any kind of oppression—they hate it just as much when it happens to other people as when it happens to them. That strong feeling is an attitude. The seed of it was planted hundreds of years ago in the collective memory and it kept growing.

Similarly, today's Jews have no family picture albums, no letters, and no diaries of those wanderers who gathered before Moses at the base of Mount Sinai and accepted Torah to live by. They don't know much about how these people lived or died. They just know, somehow, that the key to life is learning and that the word *lechayim*, "to life," sometimes makes their voices thicken with a strange unfathomable emotion.

Jews look upon each newborn as a human being filled with promise. In the Jewish way of thinking, no one comes into this world filled with sin. It seems only right to be more concerned with what happens in this world than the next. They have always had the feeling, without its ever being said, that they should help make this world a better place. These are attitudes handed down through the collective memory.

Some American Jewish families today have little interest in the fact that their ancestors were Jewish. They may go to a temple or synagogue on the High Holy Days—or they may not. They don't really think of themselves as Jews. Yet, for some mysterious reason, no matter how much or how little they earn, they donate to Jewish charities. In the Jewish tradition, helping others is everyone's obligation. Jews give, not out of a sense of charity, but out of a sense of justice. The practice of giving is in their collective memory.

Such attitudes most Jews have all their lives. These attitudes are so natural that many hardly notice they're there. That's because they are "in their bones."

(No one attitude, of course, can be claimed to be *only* Jewish. Nothing is exclusively Jewish—not even chicken soup and, perhaps, not even matzah balls. But what *is* Jewish is the particular compilation of attitudes that exist in the hearts and minds of the people called Jews.)

Put them all together—and what you have is something pretty close to a "Jewish" nature.

There's a very old joke that tells of a non-Jew asking a Jew: "Why do you always answer a question with a question?" After a moment's thought the Jew answers: "Why not?"

But it's no joke that the Jews are a questioning people. The first nation of Jewish people started, the Bible says, because of a question. "Why pray to idols?" a boy named Abram asked.

In literature, as well as biblical history, many stories tell how the Jews often challenged even God with their questions. As a Sholom Aleichem character might say:

> . . . questions that gave God some sleepless nights. They realized there were grounds for complaints against themselves; they knew they had caused God more than a little trouble. But (considering all the troubles that fell on their heads), who could blame them for asking questions?

Unique aspects of the Jewish religion are that it is often more concerned with questions than answers and more with deed than belief.

"Among the precepts and ordinances of the Mosaic law," said the celebrated eighteenth-century philosopher Moses Mendelssohn, "there is none saying 'You shall believe' or 'You shall not believe.' All say 'You shall do' or 'You shall not do.'"

"Justice, justice shall you pursue. . . ." (Deuteronomy 16:20) was not just a poetic line to the Jewish people, it was a purpose defined.

It is a purpose that has been part of the Jewish nature since the historical day the law of God was accepted for themselves and their descendants by the people called the Children of Israel.

All this is a large part of what is meant by "Jewish" nature, for a Jewish nature is made up of *many* distinct and separate parts— just as Jewish history is made up of many distinct and separate events or as the Jews themselves are made up of many distinct and separate peoples. It's quite possible for some of the same parts to be in other kinds of natures, too. It is only when you look at the parts all together that you can see how they add up to a "Jewish" nature.

Very mysteriously, the characteristics that combine to form a Jewish nature sometimes press together more tightly than one could imagine. Once in a while, they crystalize into a flow of passion and imagination—and produce an Einstein.

Just as mysteriously, this particular alchemy often helps to create risk-takers, barrier-breakers, innovators, and independent thinkers like the personalities in this book. They are men and women, all sharing the same heritage, who have been acclaimed for their accomplishments. What they did was to take something significantly Jewish from inside themselves and use it to enrich the world.

"in their bones"

They followed Moses out of the land of Egypt
out of the "house of bondage"—
and ever after
felt for the oppressed.

They heard the law of the One God
at the foot of Mount Sinai—
and ever after
shared in the responsibility
for the world.

They were driven from the First Temple—
and ever after

fought for freedom of religion
for all.

They saw the Second Temple destroyed,
the Jewish nation with it—
and ever after
carried Torah with them
and willed to return.

They lived with Torah study—
and ever after
knew that learning was a door
to all worlds,
and reasoning
the highest of skills.

They slept within ghetto walls
and pales of settlement—
and ever after
valued personal independence,
battled against social injustice,
and questioned
the judgments of the powerful.

They were seen as strangers,
seen as enemies
seen as beggars,
seen as millionaires,
seen as exploiters—
and ever after
regarded the world
with the irony that
marks all Jewish humor.

They saw exile,
inquisition,
expulsion,
persecution,
pogrom,
holocaust—
and ever after
fought against prejudice,

discrimination, and the
denial of human rights
to any people.

They smelled the smoke
of chimneys,
saw the rebirth
of the State of Israel—
and ever after
carried along
the indomitable spirit
of the Jewish people.

(Molly Cone)

2
THEODOR HERZL

"All deeds of men are dreams at first. . . . If you will it, it is no dream."

Theodor Herzl (1860–1904), founding father of the State of Israel.

He turned an idea for a
novel into a plan to save
the Jewish world.

On a Sunday in May 1895, Baron Maurice de Hirsch, the renowned Jewish philanthropist, received a visitor in the drawing room of his Paris mansion.

The caller was tall, broad-shouldered, with piercing black eyes, thick eyebrows, and a fashionably trimmed but luxurious black beard. He was thirty-five years old, a Hungarian Jew from Vienna. Like his parents, he was an assimilated Jew, with little Jewish education. No one, least of all Baron de Hirsch, would have guessed that this man would be the founding father of the modern Jewish state.

His name was Theodor Herzl.

Baron de Hirsch nodded a welcome. He had had two letters from this Herzl asking for an appointment. The first letter his secretary had answered for him, putting Herzl off. The second caused the Baron to make a little time in his crowded schedule. It had said: "Until now you have been only a philanthropist. . . . I will show you how to become more."

Baron de Hirsch was one of the few rich men of the day who felt duty bound to share his wealth with the poor, especially the Jewish poor.

He had offered 50 million francs to the Russian government as a donation to finance vocational training for the downtrodden Jews in that land, but the Russian government had refused his offer. So instead he spent the millions to build a farming colony in Argentina. His colony was meant to resettle hundreds of thousands of poor Russian Jews. To his dismay, only about six thousand had actually emigrated there. He also built a colony in Saskatchawan, Canada.

Herzl spoke up boldly. "Have you a full hour for me? . . . I need at least that much time only to hint at how much I have to say!"

"Just go ahead," de Hirsch said. He even smiled.

And Herzl plunged into a discussion of the Jewish problem.

13

He pounced upon the baron's scheme for settling oppressed Russian Jews in the Argentine and bluntly told him that everything he had done was wrong. Mere settlement could not create a homeland for Jews, Herzl said.

The baron smiled again, not so kindly this time. "What is your alternative?"

"My alternative," said Herzl, "is the establishment of a sovereign Jewish state."

Baron de Hirsch stared at his guest incredulously. Many Orthodox Jews believed, had believed for centuries, that the return to their own land would be brought about only through the coming of the Messiah. What manner of man, he wondered, could present an idea so much in conflict with the traditional belief?

Herzl got through only six of his twenty-two pages of prepared notes when de Hirsch, no longer smiling, cut off the interview and sent him on his way.

What manner of man was Herzl? Many others would soon ask the same question. For Theodor Herzl had nothing out of which to create a Jewish state except a poetic dream.

Like so many Jews in the Hungary and Germany of their time, Theodor's parents, Jakob and Jeannette Herzl, were only vaguely aware of their Jewish identity. Though Theodor's Orthodox grandfather, Simon Herzl, lived a six-hour train ride from the Herzl house in Budapest, Theodor's life seemed to have no connection to his grandfather's. When he thought of his grandfather, he envisioned an old man in a fur cap.

The Jewish subjects taught in Herzl's parochial elementary school seemed to have little connection to his grandfather either. Herzl's diary, begun when he was much older, recalls only "the thrashing I received because I did not remember the details of the Exodus of the Jews from Egypt."

As a child, Herzl hardly thought of himself as Jewish. He grew up as a "thoroughly emancipated, antitraditional, secular, would-be German boy." So removed was Herzl from Judiasm that, when he married and became a father, he did not have his son circumcised.

It was odd, therefore, that, as a law student at the University of Vienna, he had taken note of small anti-Semitic incidents and never forgot them. Odd too was his reaction to the scandalous

Dreyfus case in France in October 1894. Living in Paris at that time as a correspondent for a Vienna newspaper, he observed the mob surging at the iron gates. Dutifully he recorded their shouts, "Death to all Jews." Not death to the one Jewish prisoner falsely accused of spying for the enemy, but death to *all Jews.*

He sent off his story, but the sound stayed in his ears.

He thought about writing a book for and on the Jews. Once before he had thought of writing a "Jewish" novel. That had been long ago when he was brooding over the suicide of a Jewish friend. He had seen that friend as the main character in his novel. But now, inexplicably, he saw himself as the central figure. The hero of his novel, he decided, would set out to find a new promised land, a refuge for all Jews everywhere.

Then, almost in an instant, it became not an idea for a novel but a plan for political action. The sudden transformation mystified Herzl, adding to his excitement. He saw in his solution a vision of "immeasurable greatness."

"It has the appearance of a stupendous dream," he wrote in his diary. "For days and weeks it has absorbed me to the point of unconsciousness. It accompanies me wherever I go, it hovers over my ordinary conversation, looks over my shoulder during my ridiculously petty journalistic work, haunts and intoxicates me."

Baron de Hirsch's refusal to listen to his idea only spurred Herzl on. He went home and worked on it some more.

He was filled with a powerful torrent of ideas and plans. "Dream and deed are not as different from one another as many believe," he wrote in his diary. "All deeds of men are dreams at first. . . . If you will it, it is no dream."

He hurled himself into the job of setting down his vision on paper, completing his sixty-eight-page manuscript titled *The Jewish State* in 1896.

"The idea which I have developed in this pamphlet is a very old one," Herzl began. "It is the restoration of the Jewish state. The world resounds with outcries against the Jews, and these outcries have awakened the slumbering idea."

The book listed the practical advantages of a homeland in which Jews would never again be subjected to anti-Semitism. It detailed the needs in establishing such a state: the need for a congress of Jewish representatives, for money, for engineers, technicians, and skilled others.

Herzl planned to offer to buy Palestine from Sultan Abdul Hamid II with the help of the Rothschild fortune, but neither Rothschild nor other wealthy Jews were willing to support such a scheme. Herzl went to the Russian czar, to the German kaiser, and then to the English Foreign Office. He found no sponsorship. In his quest, he neglected his wife and children and his own health. To the day of his untimely death in his forty-fourth year, he did not cease to seek the support of monarchs, financiers, intellectuals, and the whole of the Jewish people.

He traveled even to the Vatican and asked Pope Pius X for the Church's good will and understanding in exchange for international control of the holy places in Palestine.

"We cannot prevent the Hebrews from going to Jerusalem," the Pope said, "but we could never sanction it. The Hebrews have not recognized our Lord, therefore we cannot recognize the Hebrew people."

Herzl didn't know that fifteen years before his slim book was published, a Russian Jew named Leo Pinsker, in reaction to the pogroms of 1881, had written a book calling for the creation of a Jewish nation in their own territory. Nor did Herzl know that others also had suggested the same idea but, like Pinsker, had been dismissed as lunatics or worse.

It had been proposed in the seventeenth century by a man named Sabbatai Zevi. Historians called him a "false messiah." The German Jewish press dubbed Herzl another false messiah.

Herzl's book created general astonishment. His carefully outlined proposal was called a "piece of nonsense." The German papers cracked jokes about the "Jewish Jules Verne." People on the streets of Vienna pointed and laughed at him. He was crazy, said the publisher of a Vienna weekly newspaper.

"No man in Vienna was so derided as Herzl was," wrote Stefan Zweig in his memoirs, "except perhaps Sigmund Freud, . . . who also tried, single-handedly, to create a grand world concept."

"Burn the manuscript," a friend of his had advised.

But Herzl didn't burn it.

In spite of little real encouragement, Herzl called for a world Jewish congress. It met early in 1897 in Basle, Switzerland, attracting Zionist representatives from as far as Australia. For the first time in more than 1,800 years a Jewish body representing communities from nearly everywhere in the Diaspora gathered to discuss the Jewish future.

The program drawn up on that occasion is now famous: "The object of Zionism is to establish for the Jewish people a publicly and legally assured home in Palestine."

When it was over, Herzl wrote in his diary:

> Were I to sum up the Basle congress in a few words . . .
> it would be this: In Basle I founded the Jewish state. If I
> said this aloud today, I would be answered by universal
> laughter. Perhaps in five years, and certainly in *fifty*, every-
> one will agree. The state is already founded, in essence,
> in the will of the people to be a state. . . .

Herzl was right. He was almost exactly right. *Fifty-one* years later, the modern State of Israel was born.

3
GOLDA MEIR

"One day we shall forgive the Arabs for having killed our sons and daughters. But we shall not forgive them for having forced us to kill theirs."

Golda Meir (1898–1978), minister of Israel.

*Her Russian great-grand-
mother drank tea with a
pinch of salt in it—so
she wouldn't forget the
taste of the Diaspora.*

Riding down through the Negev, the woman in the dusty car knew that no hint of the secret plan must be leaked. Success depended on secrecy.

If something went wrong, it was through the Negev that the Egyptian army would smash its way into Israel. She tried not to think of that on her way to Kibbutz Revivim which lay in the middle of the Negev. But it was impossible not to.

"You have a daughter in the Negev," a silent voice within her kept repeating.

And another answered, "There are many daughters."

"You have grandchildren there."

"There are many grandchildren."

If the Egyptians were not stopped, Revivim would be one of the first points to be overrun.

But Golda Meir, foreign minister of Israel, could not—for the sake of all Israel—warn her daughter of Israel's surprise attack plan. She could not risk taking her grandchildren back home with her to the greater safety of Jerusalem.

"There is nothing lonelier or less natural for a human being than to have to keep a secret that affects the lives of everyone around her," she wrote later in her autobiography, "and one can only do it, I think, by an enormous, almost superhuman effort."

Kibbutz Revivim was over ten years old. Yet the Negev sands stretched desolately about the little houses as far as the eye could see. A patch of grass and a cluster of flowers grew here and there. The desert was being held back by the fields of vegetables the kibbutz was raising—but just barely.

Yet the children were flourishing. Golda's granddaughter Naomi, a toddler, had her father's delicate dark features and dark eyes. Shaul, her grandson, was six months old and an equally beautiful baby.

Golda played with the children, sat with her daughter, Sarah, and Sarah's husband, Zachariah, in the shade of the young trees of which Revivim was so proud—and gave no word of warning.

21

They had tea together in Sarah's house instead of going to the general dining room. It had a slightly salty taste. For over a decade, the settlers had drunk this salty water. Everything at Revivim was cooked in it. Much effort had gone into drilling for salt-free water, but as yet there had been no positive results. Even the fields had to be watered with this water that tasted of salt.

Golda sipped at the brackish tea.

Once, long ago, when she was a child in Russia, she had watched her great-grandmother Bobbe Golda drinking tea that must have tasted like this. Only it was Bobbe Golda herself who had flavored it with a pinch of salt instead of the usual lump of sugar. Why? So that she would never forget the bitter taste of the Diaspora, she had said.

Perhaps that memory rose to Golda's mind. Perhaps it steadied her hand and strenghtened her resolve. For she continued to sip her cup of tea and let no inkling of her tension reach her family.

When she left for the long ride back to Jerusalem, a young man in charge of kibbutz security at Revivim managed to say a few words to her. "I know that you can't tell me anything," he said. "But do you think we should start to dig trenches?"

Golda Meir looked into the alert eyes of the young kibbutznik. "I think perhaps I would if I were you," is all she said, getting into her car.

The Sinai Campaign began as scheduled after sunset on Monday, October 29, 1956, and lasted for six days. The Egyptian bases were destroyed; thousands of prisoners along with great stores of arms and equipment, chiefly of Soviet manufacture, were taken. Documents found on Egyptian commanders revealed detailed plans for an imminent attack upon Israel.

Revivim, in fact all Israel, was saved from disaster.

Israeli soldiers stood for the first time at the foot of Mount Sinai. Some of them climbed the mountain on which it was thought the Law had been given to Moses during the Exodus from Egypt. When they saw the Egyptians fleeing, no Israeli felt greater joy than did Golda Meir.

Golda Mabovitz was four years old when she stood inside her house in the Russian city of Kiev and watched her father nailing boards across the front door. Even at four she knew what her father and their neighbors were trying to keep out. Her mother had whispered the word "pogrom." To Golda and her sister Shana a pogrom was a mob surging through their street shouting "Christ-killer!" It was this same mob ready to beat and stab every Jew who did not manage to hide.

The sounds of her father's hammer, the cries from outside, the terrible fright stayed with her. The fear gradually turned into something even stronger—into a kind of anger.

Why did they have to cower behind barricaded doors? Because they were Jewish, her mother told her. But that did not seem to Golda to be enough of an answer. And the anger turned into a resolve to do something about it.

The resolve stayed with her even when the family emigrated to the United States. At the age of eight, she became an American.

It was with her when she packed a suitcase and climbed out a window of her parents' house in Milwaukee to go to live with her married sister in Chicago.

It was with her when she fell in love with gentle, musical Morris Myerson whom she wouldn't marry until he agreed to go with her to Palestine to help rebuild a homeland for the Jewish people.

"Ever since I was a little girl, I can remember the small, tin, blue collection box that stood next to the Sabbath candles in our living room and into which not only we but our guests dropped coins every week."

She was used to seeing this same blue box in every Jewish home she ever visited. From 1904 on, it was with these coins that the Jewish people began to buy land in Palestine. (The Jewish National Fund was formed in 1901 by the Zionist movement for the exclusive purpose of buying and developing land in Palestine in the name of the entire Jewish people.)

All the while she was growing up in America, an almost daily tug-of-war raged between Golda and her mother.

"There's a *dybbuk* in her," her mother often complained. But her father saw in her, not so much a *dybbuk* or demon as her great-grandmother Golda's indomitable will.

Golda had no doubts about going to Palestine in 1921, though it was then a land of mostly sand and rocks. Even after she arrived in the twelve-year-old, unfinished, and frightfully untidy town of Tel Aviv, nothing—not the hard work nor bad food nor flies nor poor housing—ever changed her mind.

"I didn't really care whether we had an icebox or not, or if the butcher wrapped our meat in pieces of newspaper he picked off the floor. There were all kinds of compensations for these small hardships, like walking down the street on our first Friday evening in Tel Aviv and feeling that life could hold no greater joy for me than to be where I was—in the only all-Jewish town in the world, where everyone from the bus driver to our landlady shared, in the deepest sense, not only a common past, but also common goals for the future.

"These people hurrying home for the Sabbath, each one carrying a few flowers for the table, were really brothers and sisters of mine, and I knew we would remain bound to each other for all our lives. Although we had come to Palestine from different countries and from different cultures and often spoke different languages, we were alike in our belief that only here could Jews live as of right, rather than sufferance, and only here could Jews be masters, not victims, of their fate. So it was not surprising that, for all the petty irritations and problems, I was profoundly happy."

Despite her eagerness, Golda and Morris were not greeted very enthusiastically at Kibbutz Merhavia when they applied to join. The tough and hardworking young pioneers, who were trying to turn the black swamps of the Emek into fertile land, objected to the newcomers from Milwaukee. They couldn't imagine an American girl with the strength or will to work as hard as they did. They couldn't imagine it, that is, until they came to know Golda.

Golda Mabovitz Myerson (who changed her name to Meir at the insistence of Prime Minister Ben-Gurion when she became foreign minister) was one of the most remarkable women of the twentieth century.

She played a major part in every phase of the political and military struggle that led to the creation of the State of Israel. She was a pioneer worker on a kibbutz in the twenties, a labor leader in the thirties, and involved in the underground resistance to the British Mandatory Power. During and after World War II, she was an organizer of the illegal immigration of Jewish survivors of the Nazi Holocaust. A wife and a mother of two children, she became Israel's labor minister, then foreign minister, and finally prime minister.

In 1948, the Jews of Palestine had known there could be no Jewish state unless they were able to contain and thrust back the Arab

invaders. But, if arms could not be bought and funds for the mainte-
nance of the army secured, the war and the Jewish state were
lost.

Golda Meir volunteered to go to the Jews of the United States
for help when other leading Palestinians, making the same plea
and telling the same story, had failed.

Marie Syrkin in her book, *Golda Meir: Woman with a Cause*
(1963), recounts what happened.

> Golda flew to the United States directly from Tel Aviv.
> She left without adequate clothes or other necessities be-
> cause the journey back to Jerusalem, where her belongings
> were, was too hazardous to undertake for a winter coat.
> . . . A delay could not be chanced. Golda, lightly clad
> and with no luggage except a handbag, stepped off the
> plane to New York on a bitterly cold January day. Rarely
> had a personage—and she was obviously a personage, in
> view of the reporters on the scene—arrived so scantily
> equipped.

That didn't worry Golda. She knew she had all the equipment
she needed—in herself.

When she stood up before a conference of the Council of Jewish
Federations in Chicago, which had come together to discuss the
welfare needs of Jewish communities in the United States and
abroad, she had no written speech. Never did Golda Meir write
out a speech ahead of time. And, as she stood before them, she
didn't even have to think about what words to choose.

One of her audience later reported: "The stately woman, plainly
dressed, with hair severely parted in the middle and tied in a
knot, violated all the rules for lady speakers. We had never seen
anyone like her, so plain, so strong, so old-fashioned—just like a
woman out of the Bible."

Golda told her audience:

> The Jewish people have lost during the last few years six
> million Jews, and it would be audacity on our part to worry
> the Jewish people throughout the world because a few
> hundred thousand more Jews were in danger.
>
> That is not the problem. The problem is that if these
> seven hundred thousand Jews can remain alive, then the

Jewish people as such is alive and Jewish independence is assured. If these seven hundred thousand people are killed off, then, at any rate for many, many centuries, we are through with this dream of a Jewish people and a Jewish home. . . .

The spirit is there. This spirit alone cannot face rifles and machine guns. Rifles and machine guns without spirit are not worth very much. But spirit without these in time can be broken with the body. . . .

The amount Golda asked those American Jews to give, and to give immediately, was five times more than the grand total she had been advised she could expect.

"It was an unparalleled success story which left the professional fund raisers dazed."

In the two and a half months that Golda spent in the United States, she raised fifty million dollars. When she returned to Palestine, Ben-Gurion said to her: "Someday, when history will be written, it will be said that there was a Jewish woman who got the money which made the state possible."

But it was more than an ability to raise funds that made Golda Meir an unforgettable Jewish woman. Speaking straight from her heart, she once said:

One day we shall forgive the Arabs for having killed our sons and daughters. But we shall not forgive them for having forced us to kill theirs.

Today Golda Meir's portrait hangs in the National Gallery in Washington, D.C. Though she was born in Russia, grew up in the United States, and lived as a guest in presidents' mansions all over the world, her little house in Israel was where she truly felt at home.

4
NATAN SHARANSKY

(Anatoly Shcharansky)

"One man's act of courage inspires another, and that person's inspires a third."

Natan Sharansky (1948–   ), human rights activist and former
Soviet prisoner of conscience.

*They laughed at him
for writing letters
protesting mistreatment
of fellow prisoners. He
wrote them anyway—to
save his soul.*

"**I** was born when the State of Israel was born and it played the most important role in my life and the life of my generation," said Anatoly Shcharansky, "but we realized this only after 1967."

In 1967, he was nineteen years old.

That was the year when Israel engaged in battle with the surrounding Arab countries and defeated them in six days.

"Israel's Six Day War in 1967 changed my life," Anatoly said.

"Before '67 I was one of many of millions of assimilated Soviet Jews who looked as if we'd lost all our roots. . . . And here comes this miraculous victory of Israel after those long, hard months of alarm, of fear. In the Soviet press they had already started writing, gloating almost, that all Arab countries are together and united and the struggle against the Zionist enemy is close to the happy end.

"And then, after the victory of Israel, suddenly the very atmosphere in the Soviet Union changed. Though they treated us with the same hatred as before, at the same time, they treated us with much more respect. Many Jews found out for themselves that little Israel was struggling not only for its survival but also for our dignity, for our freedom. That's when many Soviet Jews became part of the Jewish family," he said.

From that time on, Anatoly fought against his assimilation the way the Israeli soldiers fought for their survival. He set out to make the word "Jew" on his identity card a positive force in his life.

Even though his name was a popular Russian name for boys in the Soviet Union, Anatoly grew up knowing he wasn't a Russian like all other Russians.

Because of that word on his identity card, many things in Soviet society were closed to him. He would never be hired to work in atomic weaponry, rocketry, or any advanced space program. He would never be a party leader, a state leader, or be able to serve in the diplomatic corps. It was almost certain that he would never be promoted to a high position in any field he chose.

With that word on his identity card, there was little chance that he would ever get into scientific work, medicine, or any other field that required a university education. The best universities in the Soviet Union had very small quotas for Jews.

Anatoly Shcharansky said: "I would have liked to cross out that word and write in its place Russian, Ukraine, almost anything else—only not *Jew.*"

Being a Jew had very little positive meaning to him when he was growing up.

"The very words Yom Kippur, Chanukah, Pesach, even Shabbat—I didn't know these words," he said. "They were absolutely nothing to me. And our parents who probably knew were afraid to explain any of them to us."

All they really knew was that anti-Semitism was practiced by the Russian government. It had been that way since the days of Ivan the Terrible in the sixteenth century. That was a fact of life for Jews of the Soviet Union.

Anatoly and his friends clearly saw there was no future for Jews as Jews in their country. They became Zionists, joining those who believed in the return of the Jewish people to the land of Israel.

They began to get together to learn Hebrew. They began to learn Jewish history and read Jewish books. A copy of Leon Uris's novel, *Exodus*, left by a tourist, was passed around from one pair of hands to another until its pages were falling out. They copied it line by line and the handwritten copy continued its rounds.

In secret they listened to Kol Yisrael, the radio voice of Israel. In secret they gathered to celebrate the Jewish holidays. But they made no secret of their ultimate goal—emigration to Israel.

A "refusenik" was a Jew who had applied for permission to leave the Soviet Union and had been refused. Before long, Anatoly and most of his friends were refuseniks.

Refuseniks were considered outcasts. They were subject to constant bugging, searches, and arrests from the KGB, the Russian secret police. Often they were fired from their jobs and accused of crimes they did not commit. Refuseniks were often punished for having applied to leave or helping others to leave.

All that didn't stop Anatoly. He kept resubmitting his request to emigrate.

It was Anatoly's optimism that first attracted Natalya Stiglitz, the Jewish Russian girl who became his wife. They met at one of the Hebrew-learning classes.

"When I looked at Tolik for the first time," said Natalya, "I thought—Israelis probably look like him."

It seemed to her that everything about Anatoly Shcharansky symbolized freedom. What she saw was a round-faced, very short young man, wearing a very old sweater and a very big smile.

The Hebrew class members celebrated their first Passover seder together. All Natalya knew about the Passover festival was that matzah was eaten. Much of what was on the stiffly starched white tablecloth was as unfamiliar to her as the yarmulkes on top of the men's heads. Even the names of things sounded mysterious: the bitter herbs called *maror;* the chopped apples and nuts—*charoset;* the shank bone—*zeroa.*

Their Hebrew teacher was the only one even partially qualified to conduct the seder. He read slowly from an old Passover *Haggadah,* asking others about things he was not sure of himself.

Natalya didn't have a book; there were not enough to go around. But, as she sat at that table and listened to the story of the Exodus from Egypt, her imagination carried her back thousands of years to the time of Pharaohs and miracles.

She later said, "In our souls we were living through our own Exodus. . . .

"In every generation one ought to look upon oneself as if one personally had gone out of Egypt. For us, this was not an obligation; it was our life," said Natalya.

At the close of the seder they all raised their glasses to say the words that Jews have been saying at the end of seders for 2,000 years: "Next year in Jerusalem!"

Ouside the cluttered flat in which the Hebrew class was celebrating the seder, the KGB kept its usual surveillance. Several black Volgas, the official Russian car, waited beneath the windows. When the class members left after celebrating their Passover, the agents slowly trailed after them.

Considering the delays others had in getting their exit visas, Natalya's permit to leave seemed to arrive more promptly than usual. But there was a string attached. She had to leave at a certain time and that time fell on the day after her marriage in 1974 to Anatoly.

She stared at the paper in her hand in dismay. "But I won't go without you," she cried.

Anatoly, as usual, was optimistic. "Go," he said. "It'll only be a matter of a few months. And then we'll be together."

But the few months stretched into a year. Anatoly had still not received permission to leave. And then the year stretched into another year, and another.

For Anatoly Shcharansky they were years pushing for a more liberal human rights policy. He knew he was on solid ground. Article Thirteen of the Universal Declaration of Human Rights declared: "Everyone has the right to leave any country including their own." This had been signed by thirty-five countries including the Soviet Union.

He joined a small group to monitor how his country was living up to its promise to preserve human rights. He kept in close touch with Western journalists in Moscow. His ability to speak English and his chess-player mind that could quickly sum up and analyze a situation made him a natural leader. If something happened to someone, he made sure the West knew about it. He prepared a survey on the situation of Jews in Russia. He gave up his nights of sleep to travel from one city to another, gathering information on new refuseniks or on illegal obstacles. He was often seen on Western TV, a boyish-faced, 5' 2" figure, leading reporters through Moscow, pointing out abuses of human rights.

Gradually he became the bridge between Soviet Jewry and the rest of the human rights movement in the world. His was the "voice" of the aliyah movement, the most powerful voice of dissent in the Soviet Union.

The KGB began to watch him "day and night," said poet Felix Kandel in his book, *The Gates of Our Exodus.*

> The car by the doorway. KGB agents by the door of the apartment. He was in the elevator, and they were there too. He was outside the synagogue, they were there too, by his side. Five to eight men at once.

It was no use pretending they weren't there. It amused him, once in a while, to defy them. Once, when an agent jumped into a cab with him, Anatoly paid only half the fare when he hopped out, leaving his uninvited companion to pay the other half.

Another time, when an agent stationed outside his building

was warming himself with steady sips of vodka, Anatoly rang up the KGB headquarters.

"I've got one of your men here drinking while on duty," he reported.

But nothing Anatoly did was funny to the KGB. Finally, the Kremlin decided to make an example of this thirty-year-old Jewish computer specialist named Anatoly Shcharansky. For five years he had been helping Jews leave Russia under the noses of the official police. And for five years he had been getting away with it.

Arrested on the false charge of "spying for the United States," Anatoly was hauled before the authorities.

They promised him a light sentence, a speedy release, and even a meeting with his wife if he would work with the investigators to help destroy the Jewish emigration movement. His response: a smile. He was warned that he faced a long term in prison if he didn't cooperate. He shrugged. He was shouted at and threatened with execution by firing squad.

And finally he was brought to trial.

In a hostile courtroom in Moscow on July 14, 1978, Anatoly Shcharansky called the accusation against him "absurd."

Outside the court building, the street was full of hundreds of people, many of them refuseniks. KGB men in civilian dress stood guard at the doors. None of Anatoly's friends, not even his mother, was allowed in. No one but his brother Leonid, who had only just managed to slip in and squeeze into a back row, was listening to what Anatoly was saying.

"Hang him!" hecklers began to shout halfway through Anatoly's speech in his own defense.

To nobody's surprise, the verdict was "Guilty!" Anatoly was sentenced to three years in prison and ten years in desolate labor camps.

"If you have anything to say," said the judge, "say it now."

Anatoly said: "For more than 2,000 years the Jewish people, my people, have been dispersed. But, wherever they are, wherever Jews are found, every year they have repeated, 'Next year in Jerusalem.'

"Next year in Jerusalem!" Anatoly said again when they started to lead him away. Twice in Hebrew he said it, and then once more in Russian.

At a labor camp near Perm in the Urals, Anatoly was locked up for 185 days in a seven-foot-square punishment cell.

He received food and water only every other day. In 1981 he was given three additional years in prison for "continuing to consider himself not guilty." And still he kept voicing his protests.

"One man's act of courage inspires another, and that person's inspires a third."

If the authorities placed him in an isolation cell to break his will, he would sing aloud during his days there every Hebrew song he had ever memorized. If they told him it was futile to write letters of protest on behalf of mistreated fellow prisoners, he wrote the letters anyway.

"The prisoner who writes such a letter may not save his neighbor in the next cell, but he saves his own soul."

He spent a lot of time analyzing chess positions. As a student he had been a champion chess player. At one time he could easily play fifteen games of chess simultaneously. He could even play with his eyes closed. "Of course, I can play the game in my head without a board. That really helped me keep in psychological control."

Sitting in his prison cell, Anatoly found his sense of Jewishness growing. He found himself thinking about his Jewish forebears— Alfred Dreyfus who had also been wrongly accused, Rabbi Akiva, Judah Maccabee.

"I gained strength from the pages of our Jewish history," he said. "The fact that there is a history of resistance helped.

"I was inspired by the behavior of people who had gone through the same experience and remained the way they were before. They hadn't given in or given up, and that gave me hope."

In all, Shcharansky spent 3,255 days in Soviet prisons and work camps. He was allowed only "two letters a year in a good year" from his family. The bad years were when he was punished and not allowed any letters.

He had little idea of what was going on "outside." He didn't know, for instance, that he was an international celebrity. Working from Israel, his wife, Avital (her Hebrew name), had publicized his plight to the world. Leaders, presidents, and prime ministers were urging his release.

On a February morning in 1986, after nine years of prison life, Anatoly's cell door was opened and through it was tossed a suit of civilian clothes. When he put them on, they hung on him like a father's clothes on a small boy.

Escorted by four KGB agents, Anatoly was flown to a Moscow airport and put aboard another plane. They had told him nothing.

He squinted at the sun. The plane was flying west, he concluded. Out of Russia?

"Where are we going?" he asked the agents.

"I'm not authorized to say," one told him grimly. "Only that you are being deprived of your Soviet citizenship because of your bad behavior."

So he was on his way out. After thirteen years, his request to leave the Soviet Union had finally been granted—only to be disguised as "punishment." Anatoly almost laughed.

He was grinning when he left the Soviet plane in East Germany. Two and one-half hours later, in Frankfurt, he put his arms around the wife from whom he had been separated since the day after their 1974 wedding.

Behind him forever was the Soviet Union and, with it, his Russian name. The next day Natan Sharansky, Jew, began his life in Israel.

5

ANDREW GOODMAN

"All my life I've been hearing about freedom and equality—how the individual is guaranteed these things by the Constitution, and how the Supreme Court has repeatedly proclaimed every American's right to them. But the words are illusions if things aren't so in reality."

Andrew Goodman (1943–1964), civil rights volunteer (right, with James Chaney, center, and Michael Schwerner, left, in the photo held by Dr. Martin Luther King, Jr.).

*Andy knew a belief was
nothing unless one was
willing to commit it to
action.*

The dusty blue Ford station wagon with eight young civil rights workers arrived in Meridian, Mississippi, on June 20, 1964. Twenty-four hours later, three of them had disappeared. Six weeks later, their bodies were dug out of an earthen dam.

They were Michael Schwerner, a New York City social worker; James Chaney, a Black, born and raised in Meridian; and Andrew Goodman, a twenty-year-old New York City Queens College student.

Andrew Goodman, one of several hundred volunteers in what was called the Mississippi Summer Project, had come to Mississippi with "Mickey" Schwerner and "Jim" Chaney to help Blacks register to vote.

As Congress was moving toward passing a civil rights bill, the South was bitterly resisting any change. Black kids had never been allowed in white schools. Black people had to sit in the rear of buses, were refused service in most restaurants, and had to sit in separated sections in movie theaters.

At the polls, one way or another, black Americans were prevented from voting. A favorite device was the requirement for Blacks to pay a "voting tax" or take a "voting test." The tax, of course, was impossibly high, and the test was a cruel joke, devised to keep black people away from the polls.

When Martin Luther King, Jr., a black Alabama preacher, started to lead Southern Blacks in a series of sit-ins and peaceful protest marches, Andy avidly followed the accounts reported in the *New York Times*.

When the group called the Congress of Racial Equality (CORE) broadcast their plans for a summer project in Mississippi to help Blacks claim their right to vote, no one had to tell Andy how important it was.

"Crack Mississippi and you can crack the South" was the slogan of the summer project. Volunteers were needed.

"I want to go to Mississippi," Andy told his parents one early

39

spring night at dinner in their comfortable Manhattan apartment.

Robert Goodman, Andy's father, a civil engineer and general contractor, was a direct man. "Why?" he asked.

"Because this is the most important thing going on in the country," Andy told him. "Because, if someone says he cares about people, he's got to care about this."

Andy's father was not a religious Jew. To him the importance of Judaism was not in its rituals of *minyans* and candlelighting but in its ethical thought. Often, at this same dinner table, they had talked about Jewish values without labeling them as Jewish. Prejudice and discrimination were the concerns of everyone. A belief was nothing unless one was willing to commit it to action.

A religious Jew would have said the same thing in different words.

"When the Children of Israel accepted the Torah, they said: 'We will do and we will hear.'"

First, they said, "We will do"—and second, "We will hear." They knew that understanding comes in the doing.

Andy's mother, Carolyn Goodman, a psychologist, shared with her husband the humanistic outlook of a liberal Jewish tradition.

"Before they'll take me as a volunteer," Andy said, "I'll have to have your permission."

Andy's mother remembered, suddenly, a front-page picture of Brandeis University students on a similar mission in Mississippi some time before. They were beaten until their faces bled.

Mrs. Goodman wanted more than anything to say, "No, don't go, Andy." But she knew that to Andy a fight for human dignity in Mississippi was very much his concern. He had the ability to feel what other people were feeling. And he fervently believed that all people were entitled to fair and equal treatment.

How could she say, "No, don't go"? If she said *don't go,* she'd have to say, "I lied when I said that people must act on their beliefs." She'd have to say, "We didn't mean all those things we told you."

"If we had said a single word to discourage him," Mrs. Goodman said later, "I don't know how we could have lived with ourselves." But she was afraid—even though she felt proud of him.

"When he asked us to sign his permission to go down there, I felt a mixture of fear, pleasure, and concern. But, above all, we knew, my husband and I, that to deny him the right to go would be to deny everything in life that we stood for. It would have been to say our life had been a lie, and we couldn't do that."

Andy's application for the Mississippi Summer Project was accepted.

He would go first to Oxford, Ohio, for training.

This was not the first time Andy's commitment to something deep inside himself was turned into personal action. The Mississippi project was Andy's second active civil rights venture. His first was to join with other Queens College students who opposed the war in Vietnam and were picketing President Johnson at the opening of the New York World's Fair.

Andy was seventeen and a senior in high school when he learned about extreme poverty in this country. He and his closest friend, Ralph Engleman, talked about it a lot. It was not only a national concern; it became also their concern.

Convincing their mothers that this was something important to know more about, they spent the week of their spring vacation in West Virginia. They talked to people living in hopeless towns around abandoned coal mines. They asked questions, got a lot of honest answers, and discovered firsthand that the plight of the Appalachian poor was part of a very real world.

"Andy was one of these individuals," said Ralph, "who was not satisfied with the wisdom and privileges he inherited. He had to struggle to achieve for himself. His decision to go to Mississippi was the result of a simple ability to perceive and feel social evil. And for Andy the step from perception to action came naturally.

"On the eve of his departure for Oxford, Andy not only was conscious of the danger that awaited him but also spoke with equal concern about the special risk being taken by Mississippi Negroes [Blacks] who would remain when the summer project was over. This was characteristic of Andy."

Andy Goodman's cousin, Jane Mark, said, "Andy was very much like our grandfather, and he had a favorite expression that he used. He said there are some people who are talkers and some people who are doers. Our grandfather was a doer. He never talked much about what he wanted to do; he just went ahead and did it. I think this is very much the way Andy was. If he believed in something, or if he wanted to do something, he would go out and he would try it, and he would do it without talking about it much or making a big production of it."

At school, Andy took courses in sociology and anthropology, reading about people and their societies, their religions, their ideas of justice. He brought these issues home and passionately discussed them with his father. He felt deeply involved.

Andy liked to use the words "illusion" and "reality." He knew the difference between them—precisely and truly.

He told his family that all his life he'd been hearing about freedom and equality—how the individual is guaranteed these things by the Constitution, and how the Supreme Court has repeatedly proclaimed every American's right to them. But all the words meant nothing if they weren't true.

"The words are illusions," he shouted, "if things aren't so in reality."

He went to Mississippi to help make the words of the Constitution real. That was important to him.

"Some of you will be arrested, some of you will be beaten, and some of you will lose your lives."

The words chilled Andy and many of the 175 Northern college students gathered on a campus in Oxford, Ohio. They were the first group being trained to cope with what they would face as volunteers urging and teaching black Americans in Mississippi to vote.

How to avoid violence and how to handle violence peacefully were part of their training.

One of Andy's instructors was Michael "Mickey" Schwerner, who was also Jewish. A stocky, twenty-four-year-old social worker, with a small beard and a large sense of justice, he had quit his job at a settlement house on Manhattan's Lower East Side to work for the Congress of Racial Equality.

Another was Jim Chaney, twenty-one, short, black, and bright though he had quit school in the eleventh grade to work as a plasterer's apprentice.

The day Jim joined CORE to be Mickey's aide was the happiest day of his life.

"I found an organization that I can be in and do something for myself and somebody else, too," he told his mother.

"Ain't you afraid?" his mother asked.

"Naw," said Jim. "That's the trouble—everybody's scared."

The first thing Jim did as part of the summer project was to help Mickey's wife, Rita, set up a community center for Blacks in a shabby office suite in Meridian, Mississippi. It held a sewing machine, a Ping-Pong table, and a 1,000-book library. The second thing was to go to the Ohio campus to help Mickey train the volunteers.

Andy phoned home the night he left for Mississippi. He, Mickey, and Jim, with five other volunteers, were on their way in a CORE station wagon. They'd stocked up on pretzels and potato chips, and he expected they'd have a lot to talk about on the long ride, heading through the bluegrass and the rolling red hills and the dusty cotton fields.

Andy was jubilant. A few cars had already reached the Mississippi border, he reported, "and got through all right."

The "freedom summer" campaign had begun.

They had set out at 3:30 A.M. in order to reach Meridian before dark.

"Always phone in to let everybody know where you are if you leave the office," Mickey kept telling them.

The next morning the three started a first assignment together. They were to drive through Neshoba County to investigate the burning of a church, frequented by Blacks, near Philadelphia. They suspected it was burned to hinder the voter-registration project.

Mickey told a co-worker in the Meridian office, "If we aren't back by 4:00 P.M., you start calling."

They weren't back by 4:00. After they had poked around in the charred remains of the church, asking questions, they had set out in their blue station wagon for the town of Philadelphia, twelve miles away. On the outskirts, a twenty-six-year-old deputy sheriff stopped their station wagon, arrested them, and took them to jail. Jim, the driver, was charged with speeding; the others were held for "investigation."

They were held until after dark, till 10:00 P.M. Then they vanished. Two days later, the burnt shell of their station wagon was found in a swampy thicket. Five weeks later, the three were found, six miles from Philadelphia, shot to death.

Because of his civil rights aggressiveness and because he was Jewish, Michael Schwerner had been marked for death by the segregationist White Knights of the Ku Klux Klan.

One of the murderers said: "We couldn't get at them South-haters in Washington. But we could get at them three we had. So we showed 'em." The killing, it was believed, was a symbol. It would scare the volunteers into going back where they came from.

But, upon discovery of the deaths, hundreds more volunteers poured into Mississippi. The terrorist tactics to stop the civil rights volunteers had failed.

The tragic deaths of two Jews and a Black, riding together, full of dreams for correcting the ills of the world, was a turning point in that initial battle for civil rights. Today, no Black is afraid to vote, to sit anywhere on a bus, or to attend any school.

What began in that summer of 1964, with the efforts of Michael Schwerner, James Chaney, and Andrew Goodman to help their fellow Americans gain the rights that belonged to them, finally broke through two hundred years of oppression.

In Mississippi, things were never the same again.

6

BETTY FRIEDAN

"My passion against injustice—and the chutzpah to think I could help end it—was not, until much later, focused on women or even on myself."

Betty Friedan (1921–   ), writer, feminist leader.

*Before her, the American
housewife had everything
except what counted.*

The reception committee didn't recognize her at first. The woman who had just come off the plane, in baggy white stockings and a dress with two buttons undone, was carrying a leather purse the size and shape of a horse's feedbag. She certainly didn't look like a celebrity. She looked more like somebody's eccentric middle-aged aunt.

Her brown eyes were darting over the people waiting for the arriving passengers. When her glance settled on the four women students from Wake Forest University, she headed toward them.

They stared at her. This was their guest speaker for the evening. She was Betty Friedan (rhymes with sedan), the world's foremost advocate for women's rights. Her book, *The Feminine Mystique*, was raising cries of anger as well as waves of applause up and down the country.

Her husky greeting startled them even more.

A reporter once said that Betty Friedan's voice "sounded like tires on a gravel driveway."

One of the committee murmured to another: "I hope they won't start throwing stones when she talks."

The half-hour ride to the campus did nothing to allay their uneasiness. Betty Friedan kept rummaging through a plastic portfolio and the leather feedbag she was holding on her lap. All the while she was asking them questions but didn't seem to be paying much attention to their answers.

"Hours, do you have the same house hours as men? How available are birth-control pills? What kind of punishment do you get if they catch you in a boy's room? Who administers the discipline system anyhow?"

They apologized in advance for the small crowd they expected for her speech. The lecture agency that scheduled the speaker had told Friedan to expect an audience of 600 people. The four young women admitted they would be happy if 300 showed. Wake Forest was then a male-dominated and male-oriented university.

There wasn't much of a women's liberation movement there—
not yet anyway. So far, they sheepishly admitted, there were hardly
more than the four of them.

Those facts didn't seem to trouble the feminist leader. For seven
years, since 1970, she had been making dozens of speeches each
year to anyone who would listen.

It was her young escorts, not she, who were surprised when
she stood up to speak that evening. Facing her was a crowd of
1,700 people, the largest any speaker had ever drawn on their
campus.

Courteous silence and light applause were the usual responses
at Wake Forest after a speaker was introduced. That night, the
waiting crowd was neither silent nor courteous. Male faces seemed
to be uniformly stamped with impish grins. Friedan's hosts regarded the crowd worriedly.

But Betty Friedan just stood at the pulpit microphone in Wake
Chapel, calmly looking around. Her first words erased their grins.

"Many people think men are the enemy of the movement I
represent. Man is not the enemy. He is the fellow victim."

Wispy strands of hair floated lazily about her head as she continued. "Why should men die ten years earlier? . . . Why should
man be saddled with his masculine mystique, his image as tight-
lipped, brutal, crew-cut—not able to cry out for help? . . . And
women: are they only . . . morons whose greatest quest in life
is to have their kitchen sink and husband's shirts as white as snow?"

The gravelly voice lowered an octave when Friedan went into
the subject of liberation of the female sex. "We have the rights
on paper, but what does that mean? . . . What does your university
think of you girls when they demand that you be in your rooms
when the boys are still free? . . . Obviously you aren't able to
control your own conduct, that's what they are saying. . . . We
are tired of being treated—and all those discriminatory rules at
Wake Forest say this—as sex objects."

The student audience stirred, a ripple of discomfort seemed to
be moving through it. But many students were leaning forward,
listening intently.

"This is a two-sex revolution and, when it is completed, we
will have new and honest patterns of life and profession, where
ability and not gender count."

Her strident tone changed slightly as she came to the concluding
words of her speech.

"And that man who is strong enough to be gentle, yes, strong enough, will be strong enough to march with the woman who is leaving behind her ruffles and her rage."

She didn't seem surprised when students both male and female stood up to applaud. She was accustomed to ovations.

Betty Friedan, almost singlehandedly, started what was probably the biggest revolution of all time in America. (Though it wasn't, as she said, what anyone else ever meant by revolution.)

Its essence was *equality for women:* equality in work, in pay, and in opportunity. And, to most women as well as men, that was a whole new idea.

The Jewish girl named Betty Naomi Goldstein grew up in the small Midwestern town of Peoria, Illinois, in the late 1930s. There were few Jews in Peoria.

"There was one other girl my age who was Jewish, and one boy—his mother told him he had to dance with me at dancing school, so naturally we hated each other.

"I didn't have a very Jewish growing up. . . ." she said in an interview with *Tikkun* magazine. "When I was thirteen years old, I announced to the rabbi a month before my confirmation that I no longer believed in God. And he said, 'Keep it to yourself until the confirmation is over.'"

She kept it to herself.

". . . it is only in my later life, and really as almost an offshoot of my feminism, that I have begun to embrace my own Jewish roots and develop an increasing interest in the mystery of being Jewish.

"And yet I see it was a very strong factor in my growing up in the sense that . . . it made me an outsider."

Sororities and fraternities dominated social life in this Midwestern town, Betty Friedan said. "All my friends got into sororities and fraternities and I didn't because I was Jewish.

"So being Jewish made me an observer, a marginal person, and I made one of those unconscious vows to myself: 'They may not *like* me but they're going to look up to me.'

"I think my passion against injustice came from my experience of being a Jew in Peoria."

She was valedictorian of her 1938 high school graduating class, was elected to Phi Beta Kappa in her junior year at Smith College, and graduated, top of her class, summa cum laude. She went on to the University of California, Berkeley, with an award of a psychology fellowship. But, even with all that, her primary goal was no different from that of her Peoria friends—marriage and children.

"I can look back now," she said, "and say, probably, if I had been a boy I'd have gone to law school. My cousins all went to Harvard Law School, and I would have, being sort of disputatious. But, of course, Harvard Law School didn't take women, and it never occurred to me to go to law school."

At that time, there were few women lawyers; few women doctors; practically no women scientists or engineers; no women police, mail deliverers, or taxi cab drivers. Women in politics were almost unheard of as were women in big business. No bank presidents were women, no company executives, hardly any women managers of *anything*. Whatever work they did, women were automatically paid a good deal less than a man doing the same job would receive. Most women, as well as men, took this for granted.

Though women could vote, a right won in 1920, most thought they should vote the same way their husbands did. By law, a woman could not buy a house or a car on credit without the signature of her husband.

That's just the way things were.

Betty Friedan's mother gave up her job editing the women's page of the newspaper in Peoria when she married Harry Goldstein. Like most men of the 1920s, he looked upon a career for a women as a waste of time.

Miriam Horwitz Goldstein spent her married life at home, looking after her husband and her children, as all proper married women in the early 1900s did. But she seemed to be a misfit as a housewife.

"Nothing my father did, nothing he bought her, nothing we did ever seemed to satisfy her," Friedan said.

"It took me until college to sort this out," Friedan recalled. And, when she sorted it out, it was obvious to her that her mother had been a frustrated and unhappy woman all her married life.

"But my passion against injustice—and the chutzpah to think I could help end it—was not, until much later, focused on women or even on myself."

When she married Carl Friedan, Betty believed, she had everything that was supposed to be really important to a woman. She had a husband, a home, and, soon, three children. But it wasn't long before she found she could not fill her life with dishes and dusting.

It was, in a way, her mother's story all over again.

It was every woman's story she discovered when she attempted to do an article about the experiences and feelings of her Smith College classmates fifteen years after graduation. Their answers to her questionnaire started her on a whole new line of inquiry.

Why do thousands of happily married women feel "desperate" and "empty"?

The article she wrote presenting some of the questions and giving some blunt conclusions was turned down by one woman's magazine (*McCall's*) because its male editor didn't believe there was any truth in what she had written. Another editor (*Ladies Home Journal*) took it upon herself to rewrite the article, changing its message. But Friedan refused to let it be printed that way. After submitting it to a third magazine (*Redbook*), she received a rejection letter stating that "only the most neurotic housewife could possibly identify" with her article.

Forgotten by the editors were the great American feminists of the past: Elizabeth Cady Stanton, Lucy Stone, Susan B. Anthony, Ernestine Rose, Margaret Fuller, Charlotte Perkins Gilman, and others. For more than fifty years, they had waged the battle for the right of women to vote. "It was as though they had never existed," said Friedan.

If the article had not been rejected, said Friedan, "I might never have started to write a book.

"In a certain sense it was almost accidental . . . and in another sense my whole life had prepared me to write that book; all the pieces of my own life came together for the first time in the writing of it."

She called her book *The Feminine Mystique* because there seemed to be no name for the problem she was writing about.

When she finished the five-year project, Friedan realized that, if her analysis was correct, then all the editors and all the experts were wrong. Her conclusion: a woman's place is not necessarily in the home.

"My agent refused to handle the book when it was finished, and the publisher only printed several thousand copies.

"I thought, I must be crazy!" she said.

So did many who first read her book.

In the spring of 1963, in the weeks and months after the publication of *The Feminine Mystique,* angry letters called her "a destroyer of the family," "an enemy of motherhood."

But letters of praise arrived, too.

"It changed my life," women wrote to Friedan.

"It changed my life, it changed my whole life" became the refrain to which the women's movement started up, rolled along, picked up speed, and reached women of all ages in all parts of the country and, even, in other parts of the world.

The revolution had begun.

"Jews have been very, very present in centuries of revolutions against one form of injustice or another, one form of oppression or another," said Betty Friedan.

"I wasn't the first of our people to have taken the experience of injustice, the passion against injustice which, if not in our genes, is certainly a product of centuries of experience, and applied it. . . ."

7

ELIZABETH HOLTZMAN

"But I think part of my success comes from not being daunted as other people are by conventional wisdom."

Elizabeth Holtzman (1941–   ), lawyer, politician.

*She wanted to do
something about what
was happening in this
country.*

It began early one Saturday morning. Brooklyn was just waking up. Windows yawned open. Kids, rubbing their eyes, peered out of doorways. Plastic bags of garbage, leaning off the curbs into the streets, stretched down the blocks.

Everything was the same as usual—except at the Church and MacDonald Avenue "F" train stop.

There was a crowd there—young people who were there unwillingly. Each had been convicted of sneaking subway rides without paying the fare or of scrawling with paint over the walls of the trains. And each was being outfitted with goggles, aprons, scrub brushes, and cans of special solvents for removing graffiti on New York City's subway cars.

Some Saturdays later, in Brooklyn's city parks, about twenty older offenders, shoplifters, vandals, and fare-cheaters, were being put to work raking leaves, collecting trash, or painting benches.

Not long after, a drunken driver, arrested once before when driving while drunk but let go with little more than a wave of the hand, woke up to discover that this time his car had been confiscated.

Then, seemingly all at once, car thieves were being pounced upon. Instead of getting only slap-on-the-wrist sentences for stripping stolen cars of valuable parts and selling the stuff, they found themself in jail for a year and socked with a $1,000 fine. Caught the second time around, they faced sentences of up to four years with a $5,000 fine.

What was happening?

They could hardly believe it, but the happening was a serious, red-haired Brooklyn woman whose name was Liz Holtzman, New York City's first woman district attorney.

When she took over in 1981, the new district attorney discovered that most of the people who committed minor crimes were never punished.

"They'd be arrested," she said, "they'd be hauled into court, whether it was for minor vandalism or drawing graffiti on the subway, and the judge would give them a lecture and they'd walk out of court and they'd laugh."

To them, the criminal justice system was "a paper tiger," she said. But, with the coming of Holtzman, the paper tiger showed real claws.

Brooklyn District Attorney Holtzman saw to it that not only were such crimes punished but that the punishment fit the crime. Thus the graffiti artists were set to scrubbing, non-violent offenders put to work in the city's parks, and drunken drivers and car thieves given their due.

"After a hard day scrubbing dirty subways, they'll think twice before writing graffiti or evading their fare again," she said of the graffiti artists and fare-beaters.

She was right. More than 98 percent of those sentenced to the scrubbing punishment were never again charged with subway offenses.

When someone asked Liz Holtzman, at their first meeting, "What are you angry about at the moment?" she smiled, not finding the question in the least strange.

It was anger that brought Elizabeth Holtzman out of law practice in a New York law firm to run for Congress in 1972. It was anger at the war in Vietnam, at military spending, and at national priorities which seemed all wrong that finally decided her. She felt strongly that she had to do something about what was happening in this country. So she walked away from a bright future as an attorney in an important law firm to step into politics.

She ran against the "unbeatable" Emanuel Celler, the congressman from the predominantly Jewish Democratic Sixteenth District. And she beat him.

This Jewish girl from Flatbush, at age thirty-one, was the youngest woman ever elected to Congress. And probably the most purposeful.

What helped her? "Initially I guess my will power or pluck," said the new congresswoman, "since most people didn't think winning the race was possible. But I think part of my success comes from not being daunted as other people are by conventional wisdom. I assess the possibilities and ask what can be done. And I think being willing to take chances and not always being constrained by thought of money or fame have been important."

Liz grew up in a Jewish family that took success for granted. Her parents were Russian immigrants. Her father, Sidney, was a trial lawyer; her mother, Filia, had a Ph.D. degree from Columbia and taught Russian history and literature at Hunter College; her twin brother, Robert, became a neurosurgeon.

By the time Elizabeth was four, her mother said, she announced her intention of becoming an astronomer. At six, she decided her goal instead would be geology. At eight, she was a better baseball player than some of her male classmates (like her brother she was a good athlete). But, after graduating, magna cum laude, from Radcliffe where she majored in American history and literature, she went to Harvard Law School to prepare for her career.

The ease with which Elizabeth became a strong personality in the political world amazed even her mother. "I really couldn't understand it because, of the two, Robert is the more outgoing." Elizabeth didn't even especially like being with lots of people, her mother said. She enjoyed being with a small circle of friends. She often liked getting away and doing things by herself.

She was "basically a very shy person," her staff members later said. They discovered that she was willing to talk about anything but her personal life (a fact which irritated many reporters and interviewers).

"Her shyness is real," said her brother. On the one hand, his sister had a strong commitment to the ideals and goals she held; on the other, was her equally strong sense of values about her personal life. When she became a congresswoman elected by the people, she saw herself as a public servant. But, at the same time, she was her own private person.

"Elizabeth is very different with people when there's something she believes in," her mother said. "She's not a shouter, she's not an extremist. . . ."

Though she and her twin brother were equally red-headed, they were not exactly alike in personality. She admired "his easygoing, laughing manner, his friendliness, his ability to achieve without seeming to work for it." He admired "her brilliance, her sense of justice, her tenacity."

Through the eight grades of the Ethical Culture School they

attended, through Hebrew school, through the music lessons and other lessons, through all the honors classes in their Brooklyn high school, they were together.

"We've always been extremely close," said Robert.

They even ran together for the positions of president and vice president in their junior year in high school. They won with what their teacher said was the largest majority ever known at Lincoln High School.

"Elizabeth was an outstanding debater in both high school and college," said her twin brother. "Because she never really gave an inch." She never gave up on the issues she was fighting for or defending.

Elizabeth Holtzman (called Liz by almost everyone who worked with her) began her first term in Congress with a startling public action. She sued the Nixon Administration to stop the bombing of Cambodia. It was illegal and unconstitutional, she charged, "a presidential abuse of power."

Even though she won, the decision was later reversed by the Court of Appeals. But Elizabeth Holtzman stands as the first person in American history to declare war unconstitutional. Her legal action was a triumphant one. It showed she was not afraid to challenge authority at the highest levels to preserve the constitutional rights of the Congress and of the ordinary citizen.

Challenging authority at the highest levels is what Liz Holtzman went right on doing throughout her eight years in Congress.

In the impeachment proceedings against Richard Nixon, she asked the kind of questions everyone else was afraid to ask. She was the only one who had the courage to ask President Gerald Ford if he had made a deal to pardon Nixon. She was the one who put a spotlight on Nazi war criminals living in the United States and helped create the Office of Special Investigation to seek them out.

Elizabeth Holtzman "is the reason we are here, plain and simple," emphasized the director, after succeeding in deporting sixty who carried out the murders of thousands of Jews in Nazi concentration camps.

She was an outspoken defender of human rights and the rights of minorities, including the elderly, the poor, and women.

This government no longer awards contracts anywhere in the

world that discriminate against Americans on the basis of religion, race, sex, or national origin—because of Elizabeth Holtzman.

Because of her, the United States now has laws to prevent Arabs from trying to boycott American businesses owned by Jews, employing Jews, or having dealings with Israel.

She publicized the violation of the rights of Jews in the Soviet Union, and she backed a new law that penalized any nation restricting freedom of movement of its citizens.

Because of Elizabeth Holtzman, the privacy of rape victims in federal trials was protected by law and child pornography became a federal crime. She was responsible for outlawing discrimination against hiring women in government-funded jobs.

She came "within an eyelash," the press said, of being a United States Senator, after winning the 1980 Democratic nomination. She lost by a handful of votes to a Republican in the Reagan landslide.

When she became the Brooklyn district attorney in 1982, there were almost no women in positions of authority in that division. In little more than two years, 30 percent of all executive positions were filled by women.

"It is amazing what a woman can do to eliminate discrimination when she's boss!" she said.

As district attorney, Holtzman's attention turned to the world of homicides, burglaries, fraud, drug busts, drunks, and graffiti makers.

"I find it a constant challenge," she said.

"She's very smart, and she wants answers fast," said a woman executive, who was continually fascinated, she said, by "Liz's determination to do this job better than it has ever been done before.

"She won't listen to the practical reasons why something that's right can't be done, like there isn't enough money; or nobody's ever done it before."

Numerous measures to help crime victims were put into effect by the first woman district attorney. She revolutionized the treatment of child sex abuse cases in New York State. She saw to it that a law was passed to make it easier to prosecute rapists. She sought remedies to solve the serious problems of witnesses too frightened by threats to testify, and she sought ways to end racial discrimination in the selection of jurists.

Much of this won high praise from law enforcement professionals. "Very aggressive, very talented, and works very hard."

But, when she set up a special unit to investigate charges of police brutality in 1985, thousands of police officers objected. They marched outside her downtown Brooklyn office in protest. They called her "a persecutor of cops" and "soft on crime."

Looking at her face at that moment, you could imagine her at eight, a freckle or two on her nose and a baseball bat in her hands, getting ready to slam a ball with all her strength. You could see her at sixteen, wielding a tennis racket with the same tenacity. And you could just as easily see that, as a debater or as district attorney, she had no intention of giving an inch.

To this Jewish woman who took herself and her job seriously, the shouts outside the window only told her how important it was to proceed with the investigation.

Elizabeth Holtzman's sense of outrage originally led her into politics, but it was her liberal idealism that was directing every step of her way.

And, as she said once when talking about something entirely different, "If it goes right you're responsible; if it goes wrong you're responsible. . . ."

This seems to say, in a nutshell, exactly what Elizabeth Holtzman is all about.

8
LAURA
GELLER

"Wrestling with Torah is like making love. I get close enough to be wounded—and the texts often hurt."

Laura Geller (1950–   ), rabbi (right, with Sally Priesand, the first woman to be ordained a rabbi in the United States, left).

For hundreds of years,
a rabbi was a Jew with
a beard.

Laura Geller went to rabbinical school to learn more about being Jewish.

"I felt terribly ignorant," she said.

She felt jealous of Jews who seemed to know so much more than she did.

Her earliest Jewish memory was not of candlelighting or Kiddush or even the Four Questions. It was, instead, a memory of sneaking down to the living room, after she had been put to bed, to listen to what was happening there. Her parents and the members of their Reform temple's Social Action committee were talking about buying a house as a "straw."

A "straw"? Six-year-old Laura yawned. To her, a "straw" was something you drank chocolate milk with. She crept back to bed, puzzling over it.

The next morning her parents explained. They told her about racism and discrimination. Black families, they said, couldn't buy houses in certain neighborhoods. Buying a house as a "straw" meant buying a house in a segregated neighborhood in order to sell it to a black family.

We should do this, they explained, because we are Jewish.

Years later, in rabbinical school, Laura discovered that she had learned one thing from her Reform upbringing that many other Jews had not learned as well: Being Jewish meant being involved with *tikkun olam* (repairing the world).

It seemed to her only natural, during her years in college at Brown University, to take part in the political struggles of civil rights and anti-war activities. In her freshman year she joined a fair-housing sit-in in the state Capitol building. It happened to be the week of Passover.

In protest over housing discrimination forced on black citizens, she lined up with hundreds of others on the marble floor of the Capitol building, backs against a wall, feet straight out. Her spirits soared throughout the long hours even though her stomach complained. But she did not eat the donuts handed out to the participants. She did not forget that this was Passover.

"This was a good way to celebrate Passover," she remembered thinking. Passover was the holiday when Jews celebrate the coming out of Egypt, from slavery to freedom.

At the Passover table, the story of the Exodus from Egypt is retold and the dedication to the struggle for freedom renewed—not just for oneself but for all people. What is carefully remembered is that people can be enslaved in many ways—not only by tyranny but by ignorance and fear and poverty and inequality. At Passover, Jews remind themselves that freedom from slavery has to mean liberation from enslavement of all kinds.

"We were slaves, we tell in our story; we remember what it was like for us, so we can't sit by when other people are enslaved," said Laura Geller.

"Freedom from slavery is freedom for a purpose—for Torah, for a vision of the world where the poor are provided for, not out of a sense of charity but out of a sense of justice; where we are charged to protect God's creation, the earth and all that is in it. . . ."

After her freshman year, Geller took part in a summer project in Providence, doing community work. She worked with an organizer for the Southern Christian Leadership Conference. At the end of the summer, she went along with the director and a couple of co-workers to his conference in Memphis.

"I felt *really* uncomfortable there. The convention was very Christian and very black. I felt like I didn't belong."

"You're right," her director told her. "You should be doing this kind of work in your own community."

Though it was an obvious thing to see, it seemed like a revelation to Geller. "I realized that if I wanted to make the world a better place, I could do it starting in the world of Jews."

Geller entered rabbinical school in 1971, one year before the first woman (Sally Priesand) was ordained a Reform rabbi.

"I was the only woman in my class. It wasn't a great place to be . . . there I was, in a setting where I was the only one.

"Some of the men in my class thought I was there to *prove* women could be rabbis; others thought I was there to meet a man."

At times Geller wasn't entirely sure why she was there.

In her first year of study, she began to learn how to *daven* (pray), chant from the Torah, and speak Hebrew. For the first time she came up against traditional Judaism and the ancient attitude toward women. Some of the Jewish texts she was studying had been written more than a thousand years before.

The prayer, said by a strictly observant Jew when he awoke in the morning, thanked God "that You have not made me a woman."

Jewish law ordained that no woman could serve as a witness in a religious court nor start divorce proceedings. The house of study, the court of law, the synagogue, even the board room were closed to women.

The *minyan*, communal prayer, counted no woman in the quorum of ten adult Jews needed.

Geller was struck by the clash she began to feel between "my sense of self as a woman and my evolving Jewish commitment."

In just studying to be a rabbi, Laura Geller was doing what few women had ever done before. For hundreds of years, when Jews walked into a synagogue, the only rabbi they saw was one with a beard.

So what was *she* doing in rabbinical school? It was a question that kept floating back into her mind.

In the beginning of her second year at Hebrew Union College, she began to learn a tractate in the Talmud called *Berachot*, blessings.

"I had never learned about all the occasions for a blessing— new clothes, new fruit, seeing the ocean, seeing a rainbow, being in the presence of a scholar, on hearing good news or even bad news—I was exhilarated!"

"There is no important moment in the lifetime of a Jew for which there is no blessing," she learned.

Her male classmates nodded their heads or smiled. This was something familiar to them.

"Yes! There is no important moment in the lifetime of a Jew for which there is no blessing."

But suddenly Geller found herself neither nodding nor smiling.

"I realized that it was not true. There had been important moments in my lifetime for which there were no blessings. . . ."

She remembered herself, a thirteen-year-old girl, running to tell her mother she had begun her period. It had been an important moment of her girlhood.

Why wasn't there a blessing? There should have been a blessing—because holiness was present at that moment. In her joy, she had felt it.

"I think if my mom and I had said a simple blessing—something like 'blessed are You, God, ruling over time and space, who has kept us in life, sustained us, and brought us to this moment'—I think that would have had a *significant* impact on my life and how I felt about my body. It would have been an acknowledgment of my body as a location of holiness."

There was no blessing to say when a girl gets her period for the first time. There were no blessings, either, for such moments as giving birth, weaning your child, menopause. There were no blessings for women for such times of loss like abortion, miscarriage, infertility.

Was a Jewish woman's experience, then, not a Jewish experience? The question kept tugging at her mind.

She put all her attention on the study of Torah, that body of wisdom which every Jew is commanded to study "by day and by night." In ancient times, a beginning student was likely to find the first page of his primer strewn with raisins and nuts to symbolize the sweetness of learning. Yes, there was sweetness in the learning, Geller discovered, and there was also tartness and spice.

It wasn't until she was near the end of her second year in rabbinical school that Geller came to realize "there is a Torah of our lives as well as the Torah that was written down."

She began to listen to both kinds of Torah, to grapple with them both. Mastery came slowly. "Wrestling with Torah is like making love. I get close enough to be wounded—and the texts often hurt."

She discovered there were different voices within the Judaic tradition, not just one voice. And she discovered with a startling sense of clarity that there was, essentially, only one real blessing, not many different kinds.

"It is up to us to notice God, to feel God's presence, to celebrate that which is holy in our own experience." She discovered that

God had been present in those moments of specialness in her life as well as in the lives of brothers and fathers and grandfathers "because God was present at all times." And that, yes, it was true: There were no important moments in the life of a Jew for which there were no blessings. In the Jewish tradition, the acknowledgment that God was there was in *every* blessing. That's what made a blessing a blessing.

Laura Geller felt suddenly as if she had come out from a tight place, an uncomfortably narrow place, a place she called *Mitzrayim*, the Hebrew word for Egypt. (Its root was the same as the word *tzar*, "narrow.") The coming out of *Mitzrayim* was an exodus from the narrow places that had bound her in her struggle for knowledge and growth as slavery had bound her ancestors in Egypt and kept them from becoming the people they were meant to be.

"I had understood on some level even as a child that the Jewish story had shaped my story. The coming out from Egypt, the giving of the Torah, and *tikkun olam*—the repair of the world—had formed the core of my sense of myself and my purpose in the world.

"I suddenly realized that my experience *is* Jewish experience."

Laura Geller, rabbinical student, discovered that the Jewish story was part of her story, not only in these ways, but in other ways too. "It had propelled me outside of myself and my narrow concerns into a wider universe where each of us really is responsible for every other one."

If there had ever been any doubts in Laura Geller's mind about what she would do with her rabbinical training, there were none now.

Laura Geller was the third woman in the United States to become a rabbi. She was ordained at Hebrew Union College in 1976.

Rabbi and director of the Hillel Jewish Center at the University of Southern California, Rabbi Geller was at the same time: wife, mother, speaker, and writer.

She gave hundreds of sermons to different groups on different subjects at different times. But the underlying message was always the same: ". . . that we are all part of the same struggle, the struggle to shape society so as to make people whole."

9
NORMAN LEAR

"I firmly believe in what my mother called *mentshlechkeit* (acting in a humane way)—not only for myself but for everyone in the world."

Norman Lear (1922–   ), television producer.

He heard the yelling between husband, wife, children, and in-laws in his comedies not as noise but as a "celebration of life."

A chair with its stuffing sticking out is on display at the Smithsonian in Washington, D.C.

The Smithsonian houses such objects of Americana as the original star-spangled banner, the Wright Brothers' airplane, Benjamin Franklin's printing press, moonrocks, and Archie Bunker's old, worn chair.

Archie Bunker's chair! Archie Bunker was an imaginary character on television. He was an invention of a television writer and producer named Norman Lear. So what's Archie Bunker's chair doing in one of America's foremost cultural institutions?

Once a week, every week for eight years (from 1971 through 1978), Americans of all ages turned on their television sets to view "All in the Family," chuckling at the ear-splitting arguments going on in the Bunker household.

Archie Bunker, his wife Edith, his daughter Gloria, and his son-in-law Mike (Meathead) were an ordinary family who lived in a middle-class neighborhood in Queens, New York. Archie's chair commanded the center of the living room—right in front of the Bunker television set.

Norman Lear lifted that chair right out of his own boyhood home.

Lear grew up in a Jewish household on the other side of the tracks in Bridgeport, Connecticut. His father, Herman Lear, was a second generation Russian immigrant, a not-very-successful salesman. But in Norman's home his father was king. The red leather chair was the household throne.

Norman's father sat in that chair in the Lear living room and twirled the dials of the big Zenith radio, tuning on the Friday-night fights. He sat in that chair to pronounce his opinions on the news of the day. And from that chair he would broadcast orders and prophecies and sometimes so-called promises.

"Norman, I'm going to take you to Times Square, in New York

City, where the lights are so bright you can read a paper at midnight," he promised. "And when you're thirteen I'm going to take you and your mother and your sister around the world. Pack your things because we may be gone for six months."

"King" Lear said that, sitting in his chair, when Norman was twelve years old.

Well, Norman didn't go around the world when he was thirteen— or to Times Square either—but he never forgot that chair.

When Lear moved away from home and into an apartment of his own, the first thing he bought for himself was a red leather chair. And, when he wrote the TV series, "All in the Family" (adapted from a British program called "Til Death Do Us Part"), the first thing he put into the set of the Bunker's living room was a chair like his father's.

Lear's "All in the Family" was the most popular comedy series ever presented on television. It marked a whole new era of what was possible in television comedy.

"I grew up in a family that lived at the top of its lungs . . ." said Norman Lear. The greater part of his boyhood was spent, he said, in shouting matches with his father.

In most Jewish families it was normal to speak up if you had an opinion and to speak out if you disagreed. Traditionally, discussion was a way of life among Jews. There were even such jokes about it as: Two Jews marooned on a desert island soon had established three synagogues—one for each of them and one neither would be caught dead in. Or, wherever there are three Jews, you are sure to find four opinions.

Lear believed that some of the social concerns in this country could be dealt with by speaking up and speaking out about them— good and loud. By doing exactly that, Norman Lear flouted the taboos of broadcasting and changed the face of television. For the first time in television history, ethnic humor and social comment appeared in a weekly television comedy series.

In "All in the Family," Lear gave the nation's viewers something more than laughs. He gave them confrontation with such troubling issues as racial prejudice and female inequality.

Lear gave them loud-mouthed Archie Bunker—sitting there in his arm chair, in the center of the Bunker living room—yelling at his wife, Edith, to "stifle yourself" when he disagreed with her; calling his son-in-law, Mike, a "dumb Polack" whenever Mike disagreed with him, mouthing racial slurs everytime he referred to his black neighbors or Jewish friends; and ending up in shouting matches with daughter Gloria whenever he offered fatherly advice.

"Television comedy used to act as if there were no black and white hatred in the country, no drug problem, no friction . . ." said Lear.

By pouring a strong social conscience along with a sense of humor into his television scripts, Lear changed that. He brought bigotry right into the living rooms of Americans where they could see it, hear it—and laugh at it.

Lear's vision for changing the world was through what his mother called *mentshlechkeit* (acting in a humane way). When a Jewish mother told her child to "behave like a *mentsh*" (a "real" person), she was holding up as an example the highest form of behavior. *Mentshlechkeit* was something Lear envisioned not only for himself but for everyone in the world.

Much of what he put into his TV scripts came, not only out of his own convictions, but directly out of his own life.

Phrases like "stifle yourself" came straight out of the mouth of Lear's short-tempered, bombastic father.

Throughout Lear's boyhood, his mother simply tuned out anything her husband said that she didn't like. So did her TV counterpart, Edith, Archie Bunker's wife. Like Lear's own mother, Edith was a woman born truthful. She didn't seem to know how to hate or lie.

"You think it's fun living with a saint?" Archie asked Edith in an episode of "All in the Family." "You ain't human," he said. When Edith insisted she certainly was human, Archie challenged her, "Prove it. Do something rotten."

The arguments between Archie and his son-in-law, Mike, were not too different in style from those between Norman and his father.

"I've always used material right out of my own life," Lear said. "If we're stuck in a scene, I just reach into my gut and extract something."

Admittedly, Lear's "All in the Family" was, in his words, "a little larger than life." But it was also the essence of life. He regarded all the shouting and yelling that filled the Bunker living room during each half-hour program not as noise but as "passion." Lear called it "a celebration of life."

This celebration of life presented in the bickering and loving between husband, wife, children, and in-laws was at the core of all Norman Lear's comedies. "I consider myself a writer who loves to show real people in real conflict with all their fears, doubts, hopes, and ambitions rubbing against their love for one another. I want my shows to be funny, outrageous, and alive," Lear once said.

That they were. Lear's shows were among the most watched TV comedies in the nation.

In the mid-seventies, more than half the population of this country regularly tuned in to one or another of Norman Lear's weekly programs.

"It came to me," said Lear as if he couldn't believe what he was about to say, "that I had made almost every person in America laugh at least once."

Lear, surprisingly, was a thin, rather solemn-looking man of medium height. His eyelids drooped and so did his moustache and lips. But his air of melancholy was misleading.

There was nothing sad or even restrained about his manner. He was, as one television critic put it, "an emotional dynamo," a man of sudden tears and quick hugs. And not at all shamed by it.

"I *am* shameless about my feelings. But how can you put too much heart into your work? I know I wear my emotions on my sleeve.

"I like wet people. As far back as I can remember, I've always divided people into wets and drys. If you're wet, you're warm, passionate. . . . If you're dry, you're brittle, flaky. Who needs you?"

When Norman Lear stopped producing shows for prime-time television, he didn't stop trying to bring *mentshlechkeit* into the world.

He continued to speak up and speak out. In the halls of Congress, the American way was to discuss and debate. It was the way, too, he believed, to deal with social issues in living rooms and coffee shops.

He founded "People for the American Way" to speak up and speak out against any group that made it its business to muffle or wipe out opinions differing from its own.

With a strong social conscience and a warm heart, Lear used

the medium of television and the technique of comedy to express his concerns. In doing so, he changed the entire concept of situation comedy.

Through his TV comedy series, "All in the Family," and others following it, including "One Day at a Time" and "Maude," Lear created a new American television form. He was "a trailblazing pioneer in the contemporary American popular culture."

Is it any wonder that Archie Bunker's chair sits enshrined in the Smithsonian?

10
YAACOV AGAM

"Reality is in constant change, unexpected, and so is my art. . . . Instead of stopping time, I try to express the beauty of change."

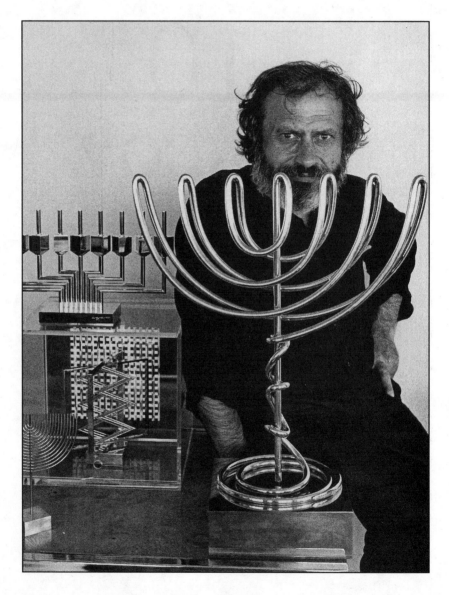

Yaacov Agam (1928–   ), Israeli artist.

*He put Jewish
thoughts into images
and created a new form
of art.*

A disk of glass that shines with a Star of David when held up to light—

A stained-glass window in which patterns appear and disappear—

Paintings that change patterns while you look at them—

Murals that seem to move over their walls or ceilings so that suddenly what you are seeing is not what you thought you saw—

Sculptures you walk through that look different from every angle—

What kind of art is this?

Its creator, Israeli artist Yaacov Agam, called it Jewish art.

"My art represents the spirit of Judaism," he said.

Nothing Agam created can be seen completely at one glance. No painting or sculpture is unchanging. "It is like life," he said. From any one place, at any one time, when you look at one of his works, "you see only a part of it, never the whole." His work, he said, reflects the Jewish view of life.

Chagall translated Russian Jewish folklore into painted images, Agam pointed out, and it became poetry. "I have put Jewish thoughts into images, and it has become a new form of art."

Many called his work Op Art. Viewers were fascinated by the fact that his works were alive, moving, transforming, changing colors, and producing new forms. They called his art kinetic. Agam liked to call his work "transformable."

Yaacov Agam, a stocky, bearded man with an exuberant air, was as full of movement as was his art. One idea bounced out of another idea when he talked, the way one image changed into another in his work. So sure of himself, he seldom bothered to be modest. A wave of his arm acknowledged the numerous first-prize awards won.

His wife, Killa, he said, was always much better at keeping track of things than he was. Keeping his accounts was something she did, even doling out his pocket money. "She won't let me keep a credit card since I've lost two already," he admitted.

Perhaps it was just as well that there was one down-to-earth member of the family. Agam's mind was always flying with new ideas. "Agams" may be seen all over the world, and they all change when touched or viewed from different angles. The bulk of his work is in museums, public places, and private collections. When asked, "Where do you get these modern ideas?" he answered, "They come from the Bible."

Born in the desert settlement of Rishon Le-Zion, Yaacov was the seventh of nine children. His father, an Orthodox rabbi, emigrated to Palestine from Russia long before Israel became a state.

"As I remember my father, he was always either at the synagogue or writing one of his books—he wrote several on Jewish spiritual values. . . . He was always fasting. He munched at night but I don't ever remember seeing him eat. On his working table there were always to be found many rare, old books of Jewish wisdom. He was deeply immersed in the study of the *Kabbalah* (Jewish mysticism)."

Agam received his early schooling in the synagogue with a *me-lamed* (a religious teacher). "But those people were very old and changed often, so I really had no regular basic training like that in the schools.

"Most of the time I walked out of the village into the desert hills, observing and following the Bedouins who lived there."

Neighbors shook their heads in concern when they saw the rabbi's young son going off by himself into the surrounding hills and dunes. They used to tell his mother that "nothing good would come of this boy."

The talk didn't bother Yaacov's father. He refused to send a child of his to a secular school. And, since there was no religious school in the village (until he himself founded one), the boy went to synagogue to learn.

Yaacov didn't mind being free to roam although he did feel jealous when he saw other children going to and from school every day. For him, Yaacov said, "the changing sky of Israel replaced the walls and ceilings of a classroom.

"I was thrown back on an inner world. I learned to use intuition, reason, and reflexes." The holy books and Jewish tradition taught Yaacov that "creation and inspiration come from yourself."

Although he had learned how to read and write, he wasn't very familiar with written forms of expression. "I used to draw a lot."

His first pictures were traced on the sands of the desert hills. He saw his drawings in the smooth sand change before his eyes as they were swept by the wind. He saw their shapes become something different before they disappeared. Curiously he watched the transformations.

He saw other kinds of transformations. "The caterpillar enters its cocoon. It is completely walled in. There is no contact with the outside world. Then one day a butterfly comes out. And then the butterfly lays an egg which develops into a caterpillar. So the cycle starts all over again."

He began to wonder—was everything, then, in constant change? The idea mysteriously excited him.

Intently he studied a passage in the Talmud where it was written that "life is a passing shadow."

He watched shadows of clouds as they moved over the sands. Nothing he looked at stayed exactly the same. Was nothing in life fixed, anchored, and unchangeable?

Like the butterfly, people were born, and people died. "For dust you are and to dust you return." Was that why Judaism extolled the wonder of life, not the worship of the dead?

"Life is a constant becoming," Agam reasoned with a feeling of wonder. "The most constant thing in life is change itself."

Yaacov was twelve when he read *Lust for Life,* Irving Stone's novel about the painter Van Gogh. "It showed me that a painting was not just something decorative to be hung on the wall but was . . . a piece of his (the artist's) own self."

Agam didn't enter school until he was thirteen and by that time he didn't fit into the regular system of schooling. It wasn't that he didn't understand what it was all about. His teachers were convinced he knew the answers. But, instead of answering a teacher's question in the usual way, he jumped from idea to idea. "Even at that stage I saw nothing as being alone in its own terms and tried to associate everything within a larger context.

"When I eventually went to study in Jerusalem, it was at a professional school of arts and crafts rather than a traditional art school."

He found that he had an astonishing capacity for drawing. But he looked at that part of his ability as "mere craftsmanship." What he was interested in developing was something he thought of as "the direct spiritual approach."

Traveling in Europe, Agam filled many notebooks with drawings.

"I went into almost every museum and important church in Italy to see the art of the past." The impact of the great art of the Renaissance and of primitive and ancient times was overwhelming, but to his eyes it represented the past and had little to do anymore with the present. "I had an inner conviction that an end had to come to this form of expression and a new kind of art had to be born."

He was mostly fascinated by original works of art. "Seldom did a reproduction, even an excellent one, move me."

Gazing at Leonardo da Vinci's portrait, *Mona Lisa*, he believed he saw what the artist wanted to do. "He wanted the eyes to follow you. He wanted them to be a smile." The smile was visible, and yet invisible. "The intent was there, but you could not quite grasp it."

The more Agam traveled and studied, the more he became aware that "even the great masters I visited were up to a point unconscious of their limitations."

So, more and more, he looked for new forms of visual expression, a new kind of art.

And finally he found it.—

He found it in the Second Commandment: *You shall make no graven images.*

For centuries, the Jews had taken the Second Commandment to mean only that worshiping idols made by human hands was forbidden. Many religious Jews saw in the Second Commandment a restriction against making pictures. Agam saw it differently.

What is a graven image? An image is what you *see*. But what your eyes see, said Agam, is only what something looks like on the outside at that moment. *"Don't fix such images into your mind"* is what the Second Commandment said to Agam. Because your eyes see only part of the reality.

"Reality is in constant change, unexpected, and so is my art," said Yaacov Agam. "It doesn't present a static situation, like a pyramid.

"The Egyptian concept of art was to petrify time, to make a pyramid in defiance of change. Time does not alter it, it stands against time and mummifies something forever.

"Instead of stopping time," said Agam, "I try to express the beauty of change." His art is Jewish art, he said, because it reflects the Jewish approach to life. "I do not make graven images."

Trying to express the beauty of change—"to capture, not a frozen moment in time, but the experience of the flux"—was the essence of Yaacov Agam's art.

His *Double-Metamorphosis II* is in the Museum of Modern Art in New York; he painted a twenty-seven-foot high mural for the passenger ship *Shalom;* he created a whole room with kinetic ceiling, transparent colored doors, and a kinetic tapestry on the floor for the Elysée Palace in Paris. It is now on permanent exhibit in the Pompidou Museum in Paris.

His six stained-glass windows, Torah ark, and Eternal Light are in the sanctuary of the Hebrew Union College in New York. An Agam mural is in the New York Port Authority Bus Terminal. An Agam sculpture, an ever-beating heart, is at the International Arrivals Building at New York's Kennedy Airport. A kinetic fountain displaying water, fire, and music revolves in the Dizengoff Square in Tel Aviv. And his sculpture *Flames of Remembrance* stands near the Wailing Wall in Jerusalem.

One of his pieces stands in front of the Juilliard School of Music at Lincoln Center, New York. Another is at the entrance to Israel's presidential palace in Jerusalem. A huge mural covers the ceiling of the National Convention Center in Jerusalem; a thirty-foot-square mural by Agam is in Birmingham, Alabama. Four of his pieces became part of the White House decor during the presidency of Ronald Reagan.

A postage stamp in Agam's image was dedicated by France; a stamp showing his art was issued by the State of Israel.

For many years, Agam lived with his wife and three children part of the year in Paris and part in Israel. Now he has an apartment in New York, too, and makes lengthy visits to the United States.

Honored on the floor of the United States Senate in 1981, Agam was extolled with the words: "He captures more than images; he captures the spirit of humanity."

But this rabbi's son who drew pictures in the sand of Israel and found a new kind of art in the Second Commandment believed that what he captured was "a particularly Jewish view of reality."

11
MAURICE SENDAK

"I am trying to draw the way children feel—or, rather, the way I imagine they feel. It's the way I *know* I felt as a child."

Maurice Sendak (1928—   ), illustrator, writer.

*Mostly, the kids he drew
were Jewish kids—
like himself.*

"**V***ilde chaye!*" the mother shrieked in Yiddish as the two small boys chased each other through the kitchen and out again. "*Wild animals!*"

To Sadie Sendak, *vilde chaye* were terrifying creatures of her childhood. She told frightening tales of the Cossacks descending on the little Jewish town where she lived, near Warsaw in Poland, before World War I.

She had crouched, hidden with her brothers and sisters, in the dark cellar of her father's store. Numb with fright, she heard the sounds of the galloping horses and the wild cries of the riders. Even after she came to America, she could hear them still in her ears.

Their father told them stories, too, of Abraham and Sarah— strange tales that seemed, like their mother's fears, sometimes both real and unreal.

Maurice Sendak was born in Brooklyn in 1928, the same year Mickey Mouse was created. His brother Jack was five years old; his sister Natalie, eight. His first hero was Walt Disney—his first love, Mickey Mouse.

Like most children of Jewish immigrant parents in the 1930s, Sendak grew up living in two worlds at once. One was the little *shtetl* world of his parents, the small town Jewish community life in Eastern Europe transferred to Brooklyn. The other was the big wide world of New York in America.

"I was a miserable kid. I couldn't make friends. I couldn't skate great. I couldn't play stoopball terrific. I stayed home and drew pictures. . . . Whenever I wanted to go out and do something, my father would say, 'You'll catch a cold.' And I did. I did whatever he told me."

Sendak's father, Phillip, was one of three partners in a dressmaking shop. "Then I was born . . . and my father lost every cent he had. But we managed. . . . I always knew my mother, Sadie, as a very scrimping woman; she was never stingy but always worried. . . .

"I remember being afraid of death as a child. I think a lot of children are afraid of death, but I was afraid because I heard it around me. I was very ill; I had scarlet fever. . . . My parents were afraid I wouldn't survive. . . . When I asked for a sled, my father said, 'You, a sled? You'll have pneumonia in a week.'"

Because of his illness, Maurice was home a lot until he was six years old. He spent a great deal of time in the kitchen with his mother, staring out the window at the children playing in the Brooklyn street below. On Friday nights he went to the movies with his mother so she could get her dish. (That was a time when a free dish was given away with every ticket as an advertising gimmick.)

His parents held the old-country notion that "pleasure was not something you should expect."

"When my father came home with good news, my mother would press her forefinger heavily on her lips and point to the ceiling as if to say, 'What are you doing? Are you going to bring the world down on us by saying something good has happened?'

"One of my father's favorite lines [which made Maurice laugh but was hardly funny at home] was: 'We're not here to enjoy ourselves.'"

Being Jewish to Sendak meant, mostly, going with his family to synagogue on the High Holy Days. Other times he hardly ever thought about it. One thing he clearly recalled was the first time he ate lobster (forbidden by Jewish dietary laws). It was urged upon him by one of his sister's friends. What he remembers about it is that he threw up.

His mother was always moving the family from one neighborhood to another. "I attended lots of different schools. I remember Sixty-ninth Street. My best friend was Tippi. She was somewhat retarded. . . . I wrote a long unpublished book about Tippi. She's a rat in it. . . . I remember 1717 West Sixtieth Street. . . . We were there two or three years, I guess. I was about nine to twelve and very overweight. Fat. But my best friend, Heshie, was fatter than I was. That's when I made real friends. . . . I knew lots of kids.

"The next place was terrible. I was bar mitzvah[ed] from that street, West Fourth Street, just a couple of blocks away, but I never saw Heshie again, or Alvin or Nini or Annie or Phyllis or all my friends. I might just as well have crossed the Atlantic Ocean."

He thought he had lost them all.

After graduation from high school, Sendak emigrated to Manhattan—"that place much visited and oft dreamed of." Except for getting high marks in art class and English, he had been, he said, a terrible student.

"The prospect of college was an absolute nightmare. I knew I was disappointing my father, who could afford, by then, to send me. . . . I took night classes at the Art Students League."

But he didn't really attend. What he did was "dodge in and out."

The first time his work appeared in print was in a book written by one of his high school teachers. It was Sendak who had done the diagrams and spot drawings. He also illustrated a book about the Sabbath, *Good Shabbos, Everybody*, for the United Synagogue Commission on Jewish Education. Marcel Ayme's *The Wonderful Farm* with Sendak drawings was published in 1951.

But Sendak didn't become much known until he drew the illustratins for Ruth Kraus's *A Hole Is to Dig*. The children he drew were sticking out their tongues, being kissed by their dogs, or sliding around in the mud.

They looked a little like the children he once knew. The more books he did, the more the illustrations looked like the friends he had once had and thought he had lost.

"They were Brooklyn kids," Sendak said. They "resembled the kids I grew up with. Most of them were Jewish. They had—some of them anyway—a kind of bowed look as if the burdens of the world were on their shoulders."

They looked that way because "I am trying to draw the way children feel—or, rather, the way I imagine they feel. It's the way I *know* I felt as a child. And all I have to go on is what I know. . . ."

Drawing the way children felt and going on what he knew, this short, shy man with green eyes became a national hero to young readers. His books, said the critics, perfectly captured the essences of childhood—its fears, boredom, fantasies, nightmares, and triumphs.

A good many adults, however, didn't like Sendak's illustrations. In his drawings, children seemed to have oversized heads and quite short legs—not the way American children really look, they said. What was worse to some adults, the children in Sendak's illustrations often looked defenseless.

But Sendak believed being defenseless was a primary element of childhood.

The first three books he wrote and illustrated had heroes or heroines who knew that "a very narrow escape is when somebody almost stops loving you."

There were people who were horrified when his book *Where the Wild Things Are* won the Caldecott Award. Given annually by the American Library Association, the Caldecott names the most distinguished American picture book for children.

"It will frighten little children to death!" said a librarian, shuddering. Many other adults agreed.

Where. the Wild Things Are was the story of Max who is sent to bed without his supper and escaped to his own make-believe world, a land of wild monster-like things.

But children weren't frightened in the least by the pictures in Maurice Sendak's award-winning book. They saw that Max *conquered* those monsters. They saw that Max, and not one of the monsters, became king of the wild things.

"When I write and draw," said Sendak, "I'm experiencing what the child in the book is going through.

"For me that book was a personal exorcism," Sendak said. "It went deeper into my own childhood than anything I've done before. . . ."

The story piled the fears of his own childhood on top of the fears so often told to him of his parents' early life. Even the title had layers of meaning to him. He confronted the *vilde chaye* of his own experience as well as theirs, all together, in *Where the Wild Things Are*.

Max's monsters were Sendak's own monsters. They were dreaded things like illness and death and cellar darkness, Nazis and anti-Semitism and Cossacks on galloping horses. Sendak had converted them, through his imagination, into enemies that could be conquered.

"Kids know and suffer a great deal," Sendak said. The kids who loved his book understood instinctively what Sendak's pictures were all about.

By putting himself so passionately into his work, Sendak has "turned the entire tide of what is acceptable, of what it is possible to put in a children's book illustration," his editor said. He "almost single-handedly opened a door on another world."

Maurice Sendak's picture books made him one of the best loved and widely known creators of children's books in the world. A longtime opera fan with a passion for Mozart, he also delighted people of all ages with his scenic and costume designs for operas. "Illustrating" music, he gave shape to the fantasies of millions of adults as well as children.

When Sendak was awarded the international Hans Christian Andersen Medal, the first American illustrator to be so honored, he accepted with a few words of his own.

In his case, Maurice Sendak said with a whimsical smile, ". . . it should be called the Hans *Jewish* Andersen Medal."

12

ISAAC BASHEVIS SINGER

"My future is my past. My fiction is memoirs, my memoirs are fiction."

Isaac Bashevis Singer (1904–   ), author, journalist.

*He wrote in Yiddish
and was read even by
Japanese housewives.*

The American who came before the king of Sweden to receive a Nobel Prize was an old man. He was small and frail with a rosy complexion and an almost entirely bald head. But, when he bowed to King Carl XVI Gustaf, the bright blue eyes held the merry look of a boy.

Isaac Bashevis Singer was seventy-four years old when he was awarded the 1978 Nobel Prize for literature, the highest honor a writer can win. It was the first time in history that the Nobel Prize was given to an author who wrote his books in Yiddish.

Into Singer's hands, the king placed a diploma, a gold medal, and a check for $163,000. To a man who had grown up poor in a Polish ghetto, who wrote stories that came out of his own life and his own imagination—this was a big surprise.

It was a surprise even though a whole wall of the study in his apartment on New York's West Side, where he lived with his wife Alma, was already covered with framed award certificates. He had twice won the National Book Award, and several times he had won the Newberry Honor Award for his children's stories.

On that wall also were almost a dozen honorary degrees, doctorates from colleges and universities all over the world. "You'll have to call me Doctor, Doctor, Doctor, Doctor, Doctor, Doctor, Doctor, Doctor, Doctor now," he had told his friends.

In a Swedish newspaper, one morning, during the week of the Nobel celebration, there was a photograph of Singer's Yiddish typewriter. He was going to get rid of it, Singer was quoted as saying. It had started to think of itself as a literary critic. He needed a typewriter, Singer said, not a critic.

Singer wrote in Yiddish, in characters that went from right to left on the page. He set these down first in composition notebooks with cardboard covers. He wrote in hotel rooms, in planes, on trains, on buses, in cars, in his study, and sometimes sitting up in bed.

Mainly, it was life in the Old World that Singer wrote about—

before the Nazis occupied Poland and herded most of Poland's Jews to their deaths in concentration camps. His stories were set in a world that vanished. His characters were people who lived in a society that no longer exists. And his stories were written in what is generally considered a dying language.

Fantastic events were completely believable in Isaac Bashevis Singer's stories. And so were demons, goblins, imps, ghosts, and dybbuks.

"All my books are about me," Singer said. "They are myself. All the events in my stories are not always what did happen but what might have happened."

In Singer's stories his fictional self is always losing things, himself included. Going to a lecture, he loses his briefcase. Going to sleep, he wakes up in a strange bed in a strange place. Walking down the street, people grab him by his lapels and won't let go until they tell him their troubles. Falling in love, he becomes entangled in complications. And everywhere demons, imps, and goblins lie in wait for him and hinder his every step.

In English translations, besides dozens of essays, articles, and reviews, Singer has published nine novels, eleven collections of short stories, fourteen collections of children's stories, four books of memoirs, and a book about the history of chasidic Jews. He has translated into Yiddish eight books by other authors, and much of his own work has been translated into many other languages.

"You don't have to be Jewish to enjoy him," a reviewer once observed. His books are read by all kinds of people everywhere from university professors to Japanese housewives.

"I was born with the feeling that I am part of an unlikely adventure, something that couldn't have happened, but happened just the same," he once said.

"The astonishment that came over me when I began to read Jewish history has not forsaken me to this day."

Singer felt right at home when he wrote about such things as demons and dybbuks. He was born in a small town near Warsaw, Poland. He was the son of a rabbi and the grandson of rabbis. Singer's father, Rabbi Pinchas Menachem Singer, came from a long line of chasidic rabbis.

For many years, his grandfather on his father's side studied the *Kabbalah*, a mystical interpretation of the Scriptures and other sacred Jewish books.

At *cheder*, Singer studied the Torah, the Talmud, and the *Kabbalah* too. For a while, he himself was a rabbinical student. But Singer, like his older brother Joshua (I. J. Singer, who later wrote *The Brothers Ashkenazi*), was more interested in writing. Like his brother, Isaac Bashevis Singer left Poland to live in the United States. (That year, 1935, Singer's first wife Rachel and his son went to the Soviet Union and later settled in Israel.)

Living in New York and writing articles, reviews, and stories for the Yiddish newspaper, the *Jewish Daily Forward*, Singer didn't get into writing novels until he was more than forty. He was sixty-two and already a world-famous author when he sat down to write his first story for children. The stories he wrote for children were the folktales his parents or his Aunt Yentele had told him when he was a boy.

Often at the end of a story, the reader seemed to be hearing the author say: "Well, that's the way life is—and you might as well get used to it."

"I am always happy to sign autographs," he told children, "because I can remember when nobody asked me to sign one."

"If a man builds a house," Singer explained, "he will know how to build ten houses. But, in writing, this is not so. He may write six books and not know how to write the seventh, which may turn out to be a terrible failure. Every book is a problem in itself. Every book demands a different form, a different technique. . . . Every time you write a book, it is a miracle if it comes out right."

But Isaac Bashevis Singer was a man who believed in miracles—not only the kind that his chasidic grandfathers sang and danced about back in the Poland of his childhood, but also the kind of magic that scientists called mental telepathy and extrasensory perception. He was always ready to believe in the existence of the occult—those secret, mysterious, unseen forces that communicate themselves to human beings.

Interviewed on a television show, he said he would give half his royalties to see a ghost.

People sometimes asked Singer if, in Israel (where he often went to see his son and grandchildren), he ever came across any of the demons that inhabit his stories. He said he found very few. "I think they would have great difficulty in Israel. They like overcast skies, old houses."

"America is my country," he said. "But, in Israel, I will tell you, I feel good. The lives of Israel's Jews are a part of my life. I can sleep well only if I know they are sleeping well."

When asked in what ways he considers himself a Jew, Singer said that he gets up in the morning like a Jew and goes to sleep a Jew, dreams like a Jew, speaks like a Jew, and thinks he has Jewish blood in him.

Probably, the most popular short story Singer ever wrote was "Gimpel the Fool." Critics said, " 'Gimpel the Fool' has the simplicity and perfection of a great folktale."

In the story, everybody is always playing jokes on Gimpel, but he hardly knows when a joke is a joke. He hears so many lies that he finally comes to believe that there are no lies. "If a lie isn't true today," Gimpel concludes at the end of the story, "it will come true tomorrow or the next day."

Was Gimpel a fool or a wise man?

"Asking an author for an interpretation of his books," said Singer, "is like asking a chicken what chemicals it used when it laid an egg."

But people went right on asking him anyway. Perhaps, what they wanted was just to hear what he would say.

He never tried to put any message into his books, Singer often said. "If we would stick with the Ten Commandments, we would have enough messages for ten thousand years."

But, regardless, many readers found a message: Jews who live by the teachings of Judaism find fulfillment in life.

Singer considered himself a religious man though he was not observant of Jewish ritual. "Belief in God is as necessary as sex," he maintained. "Whenever I am in trouble, I pray. And, since I'm always in trouble, I pray a lot."

"When he lectures," said his friend Paul Kresh, author of *Isaac Bashevis Singer: The Magician of West 86th Street*, "the best part is when he starts answering questions from the audience."

God was a creator, an artist who loved to experiment, Singer answered when asked about his idea of God. But, "like every true artist, He is constantly surprising Himself.

". . . He doesn't discuss His work. He never explains it. He never grants interviews—and, in this, how right He is!"

Talking about God, Singer often called Him "a great novelist engaged in writing the story of creation. . . . Many of us cannot wait to wake up to find out what happens in the next chapter."

Singer gave his Nobel lecture in Stockholm's Town Hall, packed with four hundred people. He started his speech in Yiddish. Then he translated what he had said into English.

He talked of the ghetto where he grew up and of his father's house on Krochmalna Street in Warsaw, which was a study house, a court of justice, a house of prayer, a place of story telling, as well as a place for weddings and chasidic banquets.

He said that, what the great religions preached, the Yiddish-speaking people of the ghettos practiced day in and day out. They were the people of the Book in the truest sense of the word. Their joy, he said, was the study of man and human relations, which they called Torah, Talmud, *Musar, Kabbalah.* He said that the world could learn much from Jews who lived as his parents did.

The evening of Sunday, December 10, after the awarding of the Nobel Prizes, when all the winners dined with Sweden's king and the queen, Singer made one more speech—a short one, this time, about Yiddish.

"People are asking me often, 'Why do you write in a dead language?' And I want to explain in a few words. First, I like to write ghost stories, and nothing fits a ghost better than a dying language. The deader the language, the more alive is the ghost. Ghosts love Yiddish; they all speak it."

Another reason he gave was: "For two thousand years, Hebrew was considered a dead language. Suddenly it became strangely alive. What happened to Hebrew may also happen to Yiddish one day, although I haven't the slightest idea how this can ever happen.

"There is still another, minor reason why I write in Yiddish, and this is because Yiddish is the only language I really know well. Of course, it's a minor reason, but it's a reason."

He went on to read a list of ten reasons why he liked to write for children. "There are five hundred reasons why I began to write for children, but, to save time, I will mention only ten of them."

But nowhere in those ten (and probably not in the five hundred) was there the most obvious reason of all.

Behind the bright blue eyes—deep inside the believer of miracles and magic—was the boy who still lived on Krochmalna Street in Poland.

"My future is my past," Isaac Bashevis Singer once said. "My fiction is memoirs, my memoirs are fiction."

13
WOODY
ALLEN

"My material was really true except
that it was exaggerated."

Woody Allen (1935–   ), actor, director, writer.

*His parents sent him to
Hebrew school to be a
scholarly Jew. What
they got was a comic
genius.*

Woody Allen has been called the greatest comic genius of this era. Fans said he was a Jewish wit who wasn't afraid to poke fun at every corner of Jewish life, even the sacred.

But many people, like critic Pauline Kael, called Woody Allen a self-hating Jew. In his films, she said in a *New Yorker* magazine review, his Jewish self-hatred "spills out."

So, was Woody Allen a great Jewish comic? Or a Jewish anti-Semite? Was it Jewish self-hatred spilling out? Or was the spilling out an excess of Jewish zeal for self-criticism?

It wasn't a question anyone could answer by asking him. Woody Allen was never like anyone else.

At fourteen, he stared dolefully out from behind dark, round-rimmed glasses. His mud-red hair looked as if it had been dried in a wind tunnel. His posture resembled a question mark. He had already grown as tall as he would ever grow—about 5' 6"—which wasn't tall enough in his estimation.

When anybody asked Allen what he'd like to be, he said he wanted to be an FBI man. "But you have to be five-foot-seven and have 20/20 vision. Then I toyed with becoming a master criminal—but you have to be five-foot-seven and have 20/20 vision."

He could always make his classmates laugh, especially the girls. Allen thought a lot about girls, particularly the ones whose bodies kept right on growing when his seemed to have already given up.

His parents never laughed at anything he said.

Martin and Nellie Konigsberg were Orthodox Jews. They lived in New York City, where, said Allen, his father was always running around doing "a million little short-lived jobs" and his mother kept the account books in a flower shop.

He spent hours in his room after school practicing sleight of hand or teaching himself to play the clarinet by listening to records. He hated school. He went in at nine, came back at three, and went into his bedroom and shut the door—immediately. He would stay in his room most of the time. He never ate with the family.

Whenever his mother passed his door, she'd stop to listen. It was as if he could see through the closed door. He could actually see his mother standing there, shaking her head as if she just couldn't believe he was still in there. That's how Woody Allen became an expert at sleight of hand. It took him endless hours, and he could still do it when he grew up.

After he became a movie actor, a writer, and a producer, he could still pick out almost any tune on his clarinet from a hum. Though he still couldn't read notes, he played with a Greenwich Village jazz band once a week or so.

He was always a little bit *meshuga,* his father might well have said. His parents sent him to Hebrew school for eight years. They would have liked him to be a scholar. That their son, Allen Stewart Konigsberg, would one day become Woody Allen, "the greatest comic genius of this era," was something they could never have imagined.

When he didn't have to go to Hebrew school (which he hated even more than secular school), Allen was usually working on something or other behind the closed door in his bedroom—except in the summer. Then, he was out in the street from 8 o'clock in the morning, playing baseball and basketball.

"At lunchtime I'd race into the house, eat a tuna fish sandwich by myself, and read a comic book—Superman, Batman, or Mickey Mouse. I'd run back out on the street and play ball. Then I'd run back for dinner, read another comic book, run back out again for two hours, come in, and watch the St. Louis Cardinals beat the Dodgers on television."

For the first fifteen years of his life, Allen said, he never read a book. "I was just interested in going out into the street and playing ball."

But, even while reading nothing but Donald Duck and Batman, he found writing school compositions easy. "There was never a week when the composition I wrote was not the one that was read to the class."

Actually, he was getting his education from the neighborhood movie house.

"The Flatbush Theater had vaudeville and movies and I saw

every comic, every tap dancer, every magician, every kind of singer. I could do everybody's act. I used to tear up the Raisinet boxes and write down jokes."

He became "Woody Allen" at the age of fifteen when he started mailing his jokes to the newspapers. He loved seeing his pseudonym in print.

He was seventeen when a press agent signed him up to write one-liners for other people. "Every day after school, I would take the subway to Manhattan and knock out thirty to forty gags for famous people to say. I was thrilled. I thought I was in the heart of show business."

His salary was $25 a week. His high school grades, he said, were "below average to way below average."

"I started to read when I was eighteen. The first thing I read was *The Killers* by Hemingway, the second was *The Bear* by Faulkner. Then I was reading everything—plays, novels, short stories, the comic writers like S. J. Perlman, Robert Benchley, Max Schulman."

After entering and flunking out of New York University and City College, Woody went back to being a full-time joke writer. It wasn't long before he was writing gags for Sid Caesar, the star of a laugh-every-second TV show.

He graduated to an apartment, an analyst, and a wife. Allen was nineteen when he married Harlene Rosen; she was sixteen. (It was the first of his three marriages.) It lasted five years.

"For a while we pondered whether to take a vacation or get a divorce. We decided that a trip to Bermuda is over in two weeks, but a divorce is something you always have."

Allen was twenty-six when he let himself be talked into doing a stand-up comedy routine in a Greenwich Village bar.

"It was the worst year of my life. I'd feel this fear in my stomach every morning the minute I woke up, and it would be there until I went on at 11 o'clock at night."

Looking back, years later, a *Time* magazine writer said, "It was a fairly unusual premiere. After all, few audiences have ever seen a man turn pale green every night."

Allen's agent agreed. "Woody was just awful. Of course, he had good lines. But he was so scared and embarrassed and—rabbity. If you gave him an excuse not to go on, he'd take it. Woody quit five or six times. We'd sit up all night talking him out of it."

Mostly, his jokes were about himself and his fears: "'I'm afraid of the dark and suspicious of the light. I have an intense desire to return to the womb—anybody's."

Or about his Brooklyn neighborhood: "The kids were so tough they'd steal the hubcaps off moving cars."

Or about his Orthodox Jewish upbringing: "When we played softball, I'd steal second, then feel guilty and go back."

Or about his parents: "They believed," he said, "in God and carpeting."

"My material was really true," he once confessed, "except that it was exaggerated."

He made jokes about rabbis: "Once, while on the way to the synagogue, a rabbi was stopped by a woman who asked, 'Rabbi, why are we not allowed to eat pork?' 'We're not?' the rabbi asked incredulously. 'Uh-oh.'"

He made jokes about death: "If man were immortal, do you realize what his meat bills would be?" or "I don't believe in the afterlife—although I'm bringing a change of underwear."

And he even made jokes about God: "The message is: God is love, and you should lay off fatty foods." And "Not only is there no God, but try getting even a plumber on weekends."

Eventually the rabbit became a real lion. Clubs all over the country hired him. The head scratching, the awkward pauses, and the anxiety became part of the act. And, after the clubs, came the talk shows, the records, and the films.

His movie *Annie Hall* won four Academy Awards.

With his movie *Manhattan*, the cover of *Time* magazine blazed "A Comic Genius." A cover story in the *New York Times Magazine* was headlined, "The Maturing of Woody Allen." He was called "genius" again in the *New York Daily News* and in the *Los Angeles Times; Manhattan* was labeled a "masterpiece." The *Village Voice* called it "the one truly great American film of the seventies."

Film critic Frank Rich said: "Woody Allen has been making people laugh by playing a single character—the archetypal urban Jewish neurotic, the vulnerable schlemiel doing constant battle against a mad, surrealistic universe."

All this acclaim seemed only to increase Allen's anxieties. Jewish? Sure he was Jewish, Allen said. But he thought his artistic consciousness was not.

Yet it was his Jewishness, a *Time* magazine writer pointed out, that had provided him with his point of view, characterizations, identity, almost his raison d'être.

His raison d'être was something that had been bothering Allen ever since he was a kid. He'd go to bed wondering, "Why am I here? Where am I going?" But he always fell asleep before he could find the answer.

"I write comically because things look that way to me," Allen said. "But I'm deadly serious. I don't watch funny movies. I watch Ingmar Bergman. He's concerned with the silence of God and, in some small way, so am I. I keep watching movies like *The Seventh Seal* or *Shane* again and again."

Although Allen called himself an atheist, he still felt, he said, "a sense of solemnity during Yom Kippur."

It was hard for his fans to believe that Allen was serious. "Feelings of alienation, loneliness, emptiness—those areas are all my entertainment meat," Allen said, and he wasn't joking.

He didn't drink and he didn't smoke and he couldn't understand why anyone would get into drugs to get some excitement out of life.

But he worried. He worried about death, not just sometimes but almost all the time. Once, when he found himself having a good time at a New Year's Eve party, all he could think of was "those shots in documentaries about the twenties where you see everyone living it up just before the montage of the stock market crashing."

He's always been that way, he said. That's why he kept going to an analyst.

Allen, his friends believed, couldn't stop being funny if he wanted to. An agent who watched Allen trip over his shoelaces on Fifth Avenue couldn't help exclaiming, "My God, he's a natural!"

But being a natural comedian wasn't all that Woody Allen intended to be. Gradually he was moving from laughs to drama. One thing that didn't worry him was that he might fail.

"It's very important that there's a certain amount of stuff one fails with. That's very important," he emphasized. Failure, to Allen, was better than always "playing it safe."

This need to reach, to stretch, to venture out, he said, "has to do with putting a value on developing and trying to grow artistically."

A good many critics thought he ventured out way too far in

his film *Zelig* (about a Jew who could turn himself into somebody else as easily as he could change his socks). At the flick of an eye, Zelig would turn himself into a Chinese cook, a black waiter, or even a Nazi follower. Cured by a psychiatrist, thus finally free to be himself, Zelig immediately married his pretty non-Jewish doctor and his image disappeared off the screen.

Was Allen, many viewers wondered, playing the whole thing for laughs? Or was he, like an ancient Bible prophet, poking a deadly serious finger at assimilation?

Perhaps, Allen himself didn't really know. Although he was a popular comedian, the author of many stories published in the *New Yorker*, and a successful film writer, actor, and director, he was still stretching, reaching, and adventuring out. Sometimes he still tripped over his own shoelaces.

And sometimes what came from his hand may have been nearer the truth than what came from his mouth.

In a scene in his film, *Manhattan*, Allen was sarcastically told that he acted as if he thought he were God. Allen answered, "Well I've got to model myself on *someone!*"

14
BARBRA STREISAND

"My grandmother called me *far-brent*" (Yiddish for "on fire").

Barbra Streisand (1942–   ), singer, actress.

People told her,
"You ought to have your
nose done," but
she wouldn't.

In boys' clothes, with a yarmulke on her head, and spectacles on her nose, Yentl fooled everyone. Pretending to be a *yeshivah bocher*, she entered the house of study, attended only by boys and men, and was soon vying with the best in the class.

Yentl broke into a world closed to women in Polish *shtetl* life of a hundred years ago. She defied tradition to prove that a woman was just as intelligent as a man.

It's no wonder that Barbra Streisand wanted to make the story *Yentl, the Yeshivah Boy*, written by Isaac Bashevis Singer, into her own movie.

Barbra also broke into a world that everyone took for granted was closed to her. This Jewish girl from Brooklyn, a wad of gum in her mouth, a squint in one eye, and a nose too large for her face, sucessfully crashed the movie world where beauty queens reigned.

Barbra Streisand proved to millions of movie fans that an ugly duckling could be an ugly duckling—and still be admired and adored. She opened a whole new era for would-be actors and actresses who didn't fit into the classic "Marilyn Monroe-Paul Newman" mold.

She won every major entertainment award there was to win—the Grammy for recording, the Emmy for television, and the Oscar for film. And she did it all without changing her name, fixing her nose, or doing anything about her crossed eye.

In the story, Yentl's father secretly teaches her the Talmud, a study traditionally forbidden to women. When her father dies, Yentl determines to go on with her studies.

"I made the commitment to *Yentl* when I read the first four words of the story, 'After her father's death. . .' " Barbra said.

Those four words reminded Barbra of her own father, an intellectual and religious Jew.

Slender, scholarly Emmanuel Streisand died when Barbra was

111

fifteen months old. Everyone thought she was too young to remember him. But she always remembered him. She knew she looked like him because she certainly didn't resemble her pretty pink-cheeked mother.

Barbra and her older brother were sent to their grandmother's house to be looked after each day while their mother went to work as a bookkeeper.

"My grandmother couldn't handle me," said Barbra. "If I was sick with the chicken pox and I wanted to go out and play, I put on my clothes, climbed out the window, and went out to play."

Barbra was a skinny and awkward child of seven when her mother married a real estate agent named Louis Kind. She shrugged him off as "a used-car salesman or something." When a cherubic half-sister, Rosalind, was born, Barbra's stepfather labeled the two girls "the beauty and the beast."

Though Barbra grew up in an apartment in Brooklyn, New York, her real home was the local movie house on Flatbush Avenue. After each Saturday matinee she hid under her seat or in the ladies' room to keep from being shooed out with the other children; then she stayed to watch the picture over and over again, dreaming of acting.

"I desperately wanted to become an actress. I wanted to express my feelings."

Her mother told her she "wasn't pretty enough, not talented enough" to become an actress.

But she kept going to the picture shows and kept seeing herself up there on the screen.

"It was *me* up there. Men were pursuing *me!*"

"She was always playacting," her stepfather said, "even when she was being scolded."

"She was always being 'different,'" a high school classmate recalled. "If we wore short skirts, Barbra wore them long. When we wore sweaters, she wore a baggy blouse. She always did the opposite of everyone else."

She was in all honor classes, yet she looked like the kids who were always in the principal's office.

"I was this absolute misfit," she said.

Barbra had been singing along with songs she heard on the radio even before she could walk. Her mother later paid little attention when Barbra and her friends sat on the stoop in Brooklyn and harmonized even though the neighbors often stuck their heads out the windows, clapped loudly, and yelled, "More, Barbra, sing some more!"

Once in a while a friend would say with surprise, "Hey, Barbra, you sing real good."

But singing in itself was no big deal to Barbra. "It's only wind and noise," she claimed. "I open my mouth and the sound comes out."

That Barbra had a quality to her voice which was unique wasn't noticed much by anyone, her mother least of all. Even though she sang in a choral group at school, no teacher ever recognized her special talent.

No one saw that Barbra had something besides talent. She was, as her grandmother put it, *farbrent*, Yiddish for "on fire."

Barbra hardly noticed when her mother's husband walked out of the house one day and never came back. She grew up and set about to do exactly what she dreamed of doing.

When Barbra graduated from high school, her mother thought she should become a secretary or a school clerk. "You'll get free vacations; summers off with pay," she argued.

But Barbra couldn't see herself as a secretary. She saved all the money she'd made from baby-sitting for a Chinese family and working as a Sunday cashier in their restaurant. Determined to be an actress, she took her savings, packed her clothes and books, and moved to Manhattan. Her mother followed. Barbra moved about from one place to another, but her mother somehow always found her.

"I was worried," said Barbra's mother. "She caused me a lot of grief. What if she wasn't eating right? What if she got sick? I didn't want my daughter dying in some stranger's apartment."

Once Barbra invited her mother to watch her act in a workshop group. Her mother watched. And then, reported one friend, "She really let her have it. She told Barbra she was a fool, she was only kidding herself. She had no talent, and no one would ever pay good money to see her on stage."

Barbra paid no attention to what her mother said.

When she told people she was going to be an actress, they'd usually say, "You ought to have your nose done."

She paid no attention to their advice either.

"We went to the same acting studio," said Dustin Hoffman. "I paid my way by cleaning toilets, and Barbra used to baby-sit for the teachers."

· He couldn't help feeling a little sorry for her when he saw her at her first audition. Eighteen-year-old Barbra, with her scrawny legs, her angular arms, her long nose, and one squinty eye, didn't have a chance, he thought.

"She was sitting on a stool," he said. And when her name was called, "she took a wad of chewing gum out of her mouth and put it under the seat."

Hoffman heard a few titters and saw a lot of smirks. But he also saw that, as surely as if she had been the star of the company, Barbra had every eye on her.

The snickering stopped when she started to sing. "She opened her mouth and knocked us off our chairs," the director said. The soaring voice coming from Barbra Streisand's throat could only be described as spectacular. Dustin Hoffman called it "magic."

"She was the most incredible performer I had ever seen, the wonder of my generation," said Marty Erlichman, who first watched her rehearse for a local TV show in 1961 and became her personal manager.

Once, after singing "Lover Come Back to Me" to a crowd that applauded with teary eyes, Barbra was asked: "How d'you do it?"

"Do what?"

"Sing like, you know, like it happened to you."

She snapped the wad of gum in her mouth and considered the question thoughtfully.

"When I was a kid, I had this wonderful bathrobe," she said. "I always used to love to come home from school and read movie magazines and listen to the radio or watch TV wearing this bathrobe. One day I came home from a terrible day at school and, like Linus's blanket, I couldn't wait till I got into the bathrobe. I looked around and I couldn't find it. My mother came home from work and I said, 'Where's the bathrobe?' She said, 'Oh, I gave it to the thrift shop.' Now, everytime I sing that song, I think of that bathrobe."

Streisand was marvelous in every performance, a director recalled, but a nightmare in rehearsals. (She had studied acting but never had any musical instruction. She couldn't even read notes.) "She had definite ideas of her own as to how lines should be read, how songs should be sung, and how the music should be performed. When she did a song, she seldom did it the same way twice."

Barbra would say: "Now, listen, at bar such and such, I'll be with you, but I have to get there however I want, and it's going to be different every time. But don't worry about it because I'll be there."

And that was true, her musical director admitted. "Her instincts were almost always right. And often her way was the funniest, the most theatrical, and we went along with it."

When he first saw her, said artist Bob Schulenberg who taught her how to use makeup, "she had bangs down over her face. And she had this little Dynel hairpiece that looked like a figure eight or a cheese Danish on top of her head, with her real hair going down her back. . . . I saw that she could be stunning even then.

" 'The nose is *there*,' I used to tell her. 'We'll ignore it and concentrate on the rest.' "

He helped her develop the first of the "Streisand looks."

The Streisand looks, as it turned out, were copied by admiring fans all over the world. And the Streisand face appeared on the covers of both *Time* and *Newsweek* as well as on the most widely read fashion magazines.

As soon as people started copying one hairstyle, Barbra switched to another. She may not have been sure which "look" was really hers, but one thing she was sure of—she wanted to look like herself and not like anybody else.

She was called beautiful and ugly, sophisticated and naive, elegant and a perfect klutz. Even people who knew her well (her mother; her husband, Elliott Gould; her admirers, Omar Sharif, George Segal, Ryan O'Neal, Robert Redford, Jon Peters) couldn't really describe her.

Many saw her as temperamental and difficult; others saw her as shy. Definitely, she was like nobody else.

Many of her habits seemed genuinely funny to some, "kooky" to others. It never failed to surprise her friends that, even when she was earning ten thousand dollars a week from Broadway, TV, and her record residuals, she clipped coupons and kept track of sales at supermarkets and department stores. Something else she did, said one producer, "was save the Christmas cards she got the year before. She'd cross out the sender's name, write in her own, and mail it out." (Today those cards are collector's items.)

A *Look* magazine reporter once kept an inventory of every bit of food that went into the star's mouth between takes during a nightlong filming. She ate pretzels, potato chips, peppermint sour balls, a hero sandwich, pickles, stuffed derma, a corned beef sandwich, coffee ice cream, roast beef on rye, Swiss cheese on white, a hamburger, a Danish, and petits fours.

When she was not singing or acting, she was often fearful, uncertain, and ill at ease. She could be defensive and defiant, combative, calculating, outspoken, demanding, and brash.

When Barbra announced her intention of making a movie of the story *Yentl, the Yeshivah Boy*, and of being the producer, director, co-writer and star, everybody in the film industry thought she was crazy—crazy, not only to tackle something so ethnic (they meant Jewish), but for thinking she could produce, direct, co-script, and act in a movie all at once. That was something no woman had ever done in the history of major filmmaking.

But she did it.

She consulted rabbis; she studied Hebrew and the Talmud. She learned about the talmudic sages and also about male-female relations in Jewish Orthodoxy.

Like Yentl in Singer's story, Barbra couldn't accept the traditional notion of a woman's place in the religious world. She felt closer than ever to Yentl.

Exploring her Jewish roots, she also began to feel closer to her father. She learned that he held a Ph.D. in education and taught English, history, and psychology in a Brooklyn high school. She discovered he was interested in drama, played chess, and was on the debating team in college. He played tennis, fenced, and was once a lifeguard.

"I look like my father," Barbra said with a strange-felt pleasure. "I have his build and his features."

Barbra made the movie, *Yentl*, a memorial to the father she wished she had known. She called the making of it the happiest time of her life.

"*Yentl* gave me a chance to create the father I never had."

Barbra Streisand has been classed with such greats as Judy Garland and Marilyn Monroe, but she had something neither had, critics pointed out. They called it "a strong base, a strong soul."

Such movies as *Funny Girl, On a Clear Day You Can See Forever, The Way We Were, A Star Is Born,* and *Yentl* earned her millions of dollars. Her single records and albums sold all over the world.

Teenagers chose her and John Travolta as their "Favorite Stars of 1978." *Seventeen* magazine readers voted Barbra Streisand and Bob Hope "the man and woman teens admire most" (1979). She was selected as the "Favorite Motion Picture Actress" for two consecutive years by *Photoplay* magazine readers. *People* magazine readers named Barbra (with Paul Newman) as their favorite movie performer. Their choice of "dreamiest screen teams" turned out to be Streisand with Redford, and Streisand with Kristofferson.

"Streisand is an original," said the editor of *Cue* magazine when she won that magazine's Entertainer of the Year Award. "And originals are rare in our industrial, homogenized society."

An original? Barbra probably grinned at that.

Only she knew that Barbra Streisand, Hollywood star, came closest to being her real self in the making of the film, *Yentl.*

15
ITZHAK
PERLMAN

"The most important part of any concert is to listen to myself *while* I'm playing."

Itzhak Perlman (1945–   ), violinist.

*His violin sang in
the ear and shook
the soul.*

Sitting at a table in a Chinese restaurant with his wife and
four kids, he looked like any other young husband and father.
His face was chubby, his hair curly. He had an impish grin, a
great, booming laugh. He held his chopsticks lightly between his
broad stubby fingers. And most likely he would be making jokes.

You might have guessed him to be a football player, a boxer,
or even a truck driver if you had not caught sight of the crutches
on the floor beside his chair and the braces on his legs.

But the couple who spotted him in a Chinese restaurant in
Iowa City made no such mistake. They knew who he was.

"We came all the way from Chicago to hear you," the woman
said breathlessly as they stopped at his table.

He gave them a wide smile and a wave of his big hand.

Everything about Itzhak Perlman was outsize: his exuberance,
his love of living, his enthusiasm, his energy—and his talent at
the violin.

"One is astonished," a *Newsweek* writer exclaimed, "at the deli-
cacy of Perlman's fingers and huge hands [they span twelve notes
on the piano]. . . . The music seems not so much played as *felt*,
spilled out in great rushes of warm, lyrical sound."

Itzhak Perlman was one of the highest paid violin artists in the
world. It was not unusual for him to perform more than one hundred
concerts a year in the United States, Europe, and the Far East.
His recordings regularly were at the top of the classical arts. He
was a sought-after guest on all the talk shows. "I've been on the
'Tonight,' 'Tomorrow,' 'Today,' 'Yesterday,' and 'A Little Bit Later'
shows," he said with a grin.

Although he had to clump onto the platform in leg braces and
with crutches, although he had to play sitting down, and even
though he had to face endless airports, hotels, and concert stages
designed without a thought for the handicapped, few people ever
saw him frustrated or angry.

"He has an easygoing, shining quality," said his friend, violinist
Pinchas Zukerman, "and it comes out in his playing."

Said a critic, "His is a type of playing that goes straight to the audience's heart."

Toby, his wife, first heard Itzhak play at a summer music camp. All she heard, she said, was one phrase of a Ravel piece and she went backstage and asked him to marry her.

That is "absolutely true," Itzhak said.

He had gone to a music camp in the Adirondacks for about seven or eight years in the summer, and "that's where I met Toby for the first time. Our first meeting was really quite interesting. You wouldn't believe it, but I played at one of the student concerts and she came backstage and said, 'Hi there, I'm Toby. Will you marry me?'"

They were married three and a half years later in 1967. Toby Friedlander was a New Yorker, studying violin at the Juilliard School of Music when they met. "But the minute we got married she gave it up. She said, 'That's enough.'"

"We are a traditional Jewish family," said Itzhak. "There is a definite, unmistakable Jewishness in our home. We aren't Orthodox and we don't keep kosher, but we're our own Jews and our children feel it. I'm proud of what I am. We all have to remember what we are, who we are, and where we come from."

Historically, Itzhak Perlman came from a long line of Jewish fiddlers. The wandering musicians in Eastern Europe centuries ago blossomed into the modern masters of today. But neither of his parents, Chaim and Shoshana Perlman, was especially musical though they both enjoyed music. His father, a barber in Tel Aviv, later ran a laundry business. Both parents, Jews from Poland, met in Palestine in the 1930s, when they immigrated, and married.

Itzhak remembers it was the sound of a Heifetz recording on the Israel radio that made him fall in love with the violin. He could sing operatic arias he heard on the radio when he was two and a half. He was three and a half when he asked for a violin.

Because he was so excited about the sounds he heard, his parents bought a violin for him. It was a second-hand fiddle that cost about six dollars.

Struck by poliomyelitis at the age of four, Itzhak was in bed for a year, his violin beside him. Later, with braces on his legs and walking with crutches, he attended the Tel Aviv Academy of Music with the help of a scholarship. He gave his first solo recital at the age of ten.

His parents didn't treat him like a handicapped person. "What my parents did was so simple and so obvious," Itzhak said. "When I was stricken with polio, the only thing they did was move from the downtown area of Tel Aviv, where there was a lot of traffic, to a suburban section. There were lots of children and a school only a block away . . . so I could walk to school every day. I practiced every day for a couple of hours, and went to school, and had friends, and so on."

Even though Itzhak, with heavy braces on his legs, could walk only with crutches, his parents didn't keep him from playing soccer with the other kids on the street. "I was the goalie. With both my crutches and my legs, I could stop anything.

"My parents instinctively did things right. They treated me in a natural way."

In 1958, when he was thirteen, he was chosen to come to the United States and then tour America as part of a group representing Israel on the "Ed Sullivan Caravan of Stars." Before the CBS cameras in New York, he clumped on his crutches to a chair, was handed his violin, and played "The Flight of the Bumble Bee" and a few other short pieces.

He and his mother traveled with the tour for two months. "We were still kosher then, so we lived on nothing but bread and butter and sardines. I'll never forget when we hit Los Angeles and found a Jewish delicatessen."

They ended up in New York, where Itzhak's father came to join them, and stayed there so Itzhak could study "seriously," as he said, at Juilliard. His teachers, Dorothy DeLay and Ivan Galamian, the best violin teachers at the Juilliard School, were also considered the greatest teachers of the time.

"What set Itzhak apart from the beginning was his sheer talent and enormous imagination," said DeLay. "I always had the feeling that he absorbed everything that I ever said to him." She taught him more than the violin. She took him to museums, advised his parents to give him painting lessons, taught him how to drive. (He later drove a Volvo with hand controls.)

During his first years in America, besides doing schoolwork, studying music, and practicing, he supported the family by playing for Jewish fund-raising dinners. "I would perform around 11:30 or midnight, after the fund-raising part, and I was up against the sound of waiters collecting the forks." He called it "terrific training."

His entry into the real concert world began with an unexpected splash.

With a 200-year-old Guarnerius violin lent by the Juilliard School, Itzhak entered the Leventritt Competition in 1964. He was nineteen years old. To the winner went a $1,000 cash prize—plus the opportunity to appear with the New York Philharmonic and other leading American orchestras. Itzhak won over nineteen other contestants, all older than he was. But, when he laid the borrowed violin down while taking his bows, it disappeared.

The Guarnerius turned up the next day in a shabby Times Square pawnshop. (The shopkeeper had paid $15 for it.) The story made the *New York Times*, front page news. It was even bigger news than when, years later, he began playing on a Stradivarius made in 1714 and valued at something over $400,000.

Itzhak returned to Israel for the first time seven years after he had left—on a concert tour which took him up and down the small country.

"The feeling was quite indescribable. You feel this is really my country. Even just landing and going into the terminal in Tel Aviv. And the smells . . . you can't describe what it smells like. But it smells like your country. I remember this when I was a kid. That's what I smelled." ("It hits me every time," Perlman said many years later.)

He played eight concerts in his native land, a nation overflowing with fiddlers. As *Time* magazine described it:

> At Tel Aviv's Mann Auditorium, Perlman played the Sibelius and Tchaikovsky concertos. Hunching forward, lips pursed, he coaxed an exceptionally warm and blooming tone from his instrument with his dancing, stubby fingers and vigorous strokes of the bow. Afterwards the audience of 2,500 cheered for fifteen minutes and shouted for an encore, something they rarely ask.

Itzhak Perlman was "already a master," a reviewer reported. Another placed him "in the front row of the very few great violinists of our day." His playing "sings in the ear and shakes the soul," said still another.

"Even if I play a piece fifty times, I always find new things in it," Perlman once said. "The most important part of any concert is to listen to myself *while* I'm playing."

"Listening to himself" has carried Itzhak Perlman to the very top of the musical world.

He dazzled not only audiences but other master violinists too. Isaac Stern became his mentor ("His talent is utterly limitless."), Pinchas Zukerman, his admirer and friend. Zubin Mehta, conductor of the New York Philharmonic, said, "It is a great pleasure to accompany him. He molds his own voice so close to the orchestra's. The result is intensive music making."

A concert violinist, Jascha Heifetz once said, must have "the nerves of a bullfighter, the vitality of a woman who runs a nightclub, and the concentration of a Buddhist monk."

Add to that, said a friend, "the antic soul of a born ham and you have Itzhak Perlman. . . . Perlman loves to show off." His humor is ever-ready. Once, at a cookout party, he played "Turkey in the Straw" with a borrowed fiddle at a rate "just this side of the speed of sound." He once entertained guests in his home by "singing" famous arias, using "mamma mia" as the only lyrics and a voice that ranged from falsetto to basso profundo. Clowning as a guest on *Sesame Street,* he announced: "I realized my dream— I got to play with Oscar the Grouch."

He was asked back to the *Sesame Street* show time and time again. Seeing him on TV, it was hard to realize that this cherubic-faced fellow with the big grin was *the* Itzhak Perlman, a world-famous violinist.

"I could probably book him every day of the year," his manager said with a grin, "but he won't play on the High Holy Days or his children's birthdays."

At his home, an eleven-room New York City apartment (without the *mezuzah* on the door, it was once the home of baseball's famed Babe Ruth), Itzhak was often to be found performing in the kitchen—fixing lunch. He liked to be accompanied by the children, playing noisily around him, and the phone, constantly ringing.

"If you're not careful," he said, "the children will grow up on you and you'll miss the most glorious part of life."

As his fame grew, Perlman used it to help make the world a better place for others. "Try getting a wheelchair into the bathroom of an airplane," he said when he campaigned to make airplanes less of a problem for the disabled. He served on the boards of hospitals for severely handicapped children both in the United States and Israel. He appeared on TV shows to talk about the disabled in cities in which he gave a concert. He gave benefit concerts. He visited handicapped children in hospitals. He obligingly made his violin moo and twitter for them, and he took apart his bow to show the horse hair. Picking up the tune of a song they liked, any song, he accompanied them on his violin as they sang.

His love of playing was as irresistible as his "great booming bass-baritone laugh."

In spite of his braces and crutches, this short, huskily built man with blue eyes and curly, dark hair was as comfortable playing before audiences as he was joking with friends or sitting and laughing with children.

Almost no one who has been to a Perlman concert ever forgets it. The lights go down. Across the stage comes a short, smiling person on crutches, preceded by his pianist carrying his Stradivarius. Perlman bows briefly, settles himself onto a seat, drops the crutches by his chair, and is handed the violin. He tucks it under his chin and tunes it, very briefly, and begins to play. Suddenly the violin has become part of him. Perlman communicates what only the greatest artists have: a love of playing—and it is irresistible.

Itzhak Perlman never thought of himself as "handicapped." When he thought of himself at all, it was as a fiddler, an Israeli, and a Jew.

16
MYRIAM MENDILOW

"I want you to learn two words: 'I care.' Caring is the basis of all civilization."

Myriam Mendilow (1910–   ), teacher, founder of "Lifeline for the Old" (with a young volunteer and one of the elderly).

*She taught that
tzedakah (charity)
came from the word
tzedek (justice).*

Mrs. Mendilow couldn't sleep. The night sounds from the street below had been shut out somewhat by closing the window. The papers she had brought home with her lay graded on her kitchen table. The soup she had cooked ahead for her dinner the next day sat, ready, on the back of the stove. But the problem on her mind could not be so easily dispatched.

For twenty years Myriam Mendilow had been teaching school in the section of Jerusalem which bordered the Jewish outdoor market. Almost every day of the twenty years, she had walked to school.

"Every day I used to see old people, many of them beggars, sitting listlessly near my school, neglected, in rags, and waiting to die."

Like old people almost everywhere, they had nothing much to do all day and nowhere in particular to go. Their uselessness seemed to weigh on them like too-heavy cloaks. They moved with their heads bent and their shoulders bowed and sat, a good part of the time, with chins sunk into their necks.

All this distressed her, and what distressed her too was the attitude toward the old she found among her pupils.

Many of her pupils were children who had no grandparents. Their parents were survivors of pogroms and of the Holocaust. They had no older people in the family. Her children needed to see old people they could respect and care about. But the only elderly her pupils saw were the ones they passed daily on their way to school.

"The constant sight of these useless and unsavory-looking people bred a lack of respect and callousness in my pupils."

"They smell!" her pupils told her.

What could she do, she pondered, what would help to teach her pupils to respect and value the older generation?

Nothing came to mind. Nothing at all.

Hopefully, she took her fourth graders on a visit to a nursing home but what they saw there didn't teach them anything. They stood about staring at the old people sitting about. They wrinkled their noses at the smells of antiseptics, medicines, drugs, and sloppily washed floors.

Their teacher kept talking to them about caring and respect. Myriam Mendilow was not one who gave up easily on anything she considered important.

Noticing that one old woman sat all day swatting flies, Mrs. Mendilow took a can of insecticide with her on their next visit. But, when she aimed the spray at the insects, the old person only yelled at her.

"What's the matter with you! What are you doing?"

The teacher held out the can of insect spray. "This will get rid of the flies for you," she explained.

The old woman pushed the can away. "What do I need that for? I can swat them myself. What else do I have to do?"

The teacher pushed the can of spray deep into her bag. She felt, for some reason, a little ashamed, as if she had given a gift that wasn't good enough. But why she should feel this way she didn't know.

She herded her children together and led them back to school. And, while her pupils were writing their lessons, the teacher sat at her desk, staring at her clasped hands, thinking.

What had the old woman said? *"What else do I have to do?"*

Swatting flies was probably the thing that kept her alive. It gave her something to do.

Something to do. The words went around and around in the teacher's head. All those people sitting in their chairs in the nursing home, all those elderly persons shuffling up and down the street— doing nothing. *Feeling* like nothing.

"Living is doing." The words came out of her mouth in a loud, firm tone. They shattered the quiet of the room like a stone through the window. The children looked up startled. Waving them back to their work, Myriam Mendilow took a long, deep breath.

How simple! she thought. The answer was so simple that she wondered why she—or someone—had not thought of it before.

To be is to do.

Myriam Mendilow was in her late forties when she gave up her teaching job. Instead, she put her time into starting a number of clubs for neglected old and disabled men and women. When she heard, at first hand, of the misery and hopelessness of so many without families, she founded a unique center based on an ancient Jewish concept called *tzedakah*.

According to Maimonides, a twelfth-century rabbinical scholar, the highest level of charity was to help people to help themselves.

And that is exactly what Myriam Mendilow did.

Her "Lifeline for the Old" started with a single workshop where the elderly and disabled were trained to repair children's worn-out schoolbooks. This developed into an entire complex including a day center. It gave more than 450 Jerusalem residents—Jews, Christians, and Moslems—a reason for living.

Life and work were partners at "Lifeline." "God give me work while I live and life while I work" was the motto.

"Lifeline" was housed in an old Arab structure in one of the poorest parts of Jerusalem, the Musrara quarter. Before 1967, it was on the border between Israel and Jordan. A sprawling building, the original was renovated and additional rooms were added over the years. It grew to include fourteen workshops, a day center, a luncheon club, and a hot meals-on-wheels service for the housebound.

"We don't buy anything," said the former school teacher whom everybody called simply Myriam. "We take in things that people throw away and a retired carpenter who works here repairs them."

At "Lifeline," no one sat around and swatted flies. Everyone worked.

They worked at bookbinding, box-making, metal work, jewelry-making, weaving, macrame, sewing, picture-framing, candle-holder-carving, and other crafts. They wrote poetry, painted, baked sweet rolls for the morning tea or cakes for Shabbat. They crocheted shawls, hand-knitted infant clothes, embroidered dresses for little girls, and made sweaters for all ages. And they got paid for it.

"At 'Lifeline' even those who are unable to work feel that they are working," said Myriam, "and all are paid the same token sum, irrespective of their productivity."

"Lifeline" products were sold in the "Lifeline" shop and customers came in and out all day. It was easy to see why "Lifeline" products won first prize in an arts and crafts show in Germany.

A staff of approximately fifty part-time persons, including many volunteers, handled things under Myriam's direction.

When school children visited and asked what they could do, Myriam told them, "I want you to learn two words: 'I care.' Caring is the basis of all civilization. If you care for others, you will know best how to behave."

No one had to tell the school children who came to visit the elderly at "Lifeline" about how to behave. They trooped from one workshop room to another, looking in and asking questions. They gathered around the old woman making a bracelet or the old man carving a candlestick to talk to them. They listened to their stories.

"Once a girl as pretty as you was in love with me," an elderly gentleman told a teenager. "But she got mad at me. She told me to send back her picture."

"So did you?" asked an eager listener.

"Sure I did," said the old man. "I sent her an album of pictures and told her to pick her own because I forgot which one she was."

Laughter. At "Lifeline," young laughter mixed often with the old. At some moments, visitors and regulars seemed the same age. Even the chronic complainers complained with a lift in their voices.

"Dignity," said Myriam Mendilow, "is the ultimate source of the will to live."

Each person discovered at "Lifeline" that someone cared about him or her. Part of this feeling came from being productive. But part also came from the services the center provided.

There were hot showers and laundry and mending facilities. ("So that the young would not shun the elderly on the pretext that they smelled bad," explained Myriam.) There was a shoemaker, a thrift shop, a dentist, an orthopedist, an optometrist, a chiropodist, and a general practitioner.

Charity? No, not charity in the sense of a handout. Half the money to run "Lifeline" was contributed by private donations with some help from the government and municipal sources; the other half came from profits from the craft shops. The elderly came there to work and they paid a small fee for each of the services they used.

"It is a matter of dignity," Myriam said.

It's—*tzedakah.*

17
HELENA RUBINSTEIN

"My fortune comes from women and should benefit them and their children. . . ."

Helena Rubinstein (1870–1965), founder of today's beauty and cosmetic business, philanthropist.

*She carried her lunch in
a brown paper bag, but
she gave away millions
of dollars.*

She was short (4′10″) and had straight black hair which, most of her life, she wore pulled back severely from a high forehead and gathered in a knot at the back.

She was the oldest of eight daughters of a middle-class Jewish family in Cracow, Poland, had little business experience, and no money. But, by the time half of her life had gone by, she was one of the ten richest women in the world.

What was most unusual about Helena Rubinstein was that she made her fortune herself.

In 1902, at the age of eighteen, dressed in a white pleated dress, a large straw hat, high-heeled button shoes, and, of course, carrying a parasol, she stepped from the train to the gasps of her Australian relatives. They couldn't stop staring at her.

The shoes, they noted, were completely impractical for the rough Austrialian terrain. And the parasol, well, when she held it over her head in the correct European manner, it did nothing to keep the swirling dust out of her eyes.

"Your father?" her Australian uncle inquired, giving her a peck on her cheek. "Your mother?"

"They're fine," she said.

She didn't mention that the atmosphere between her and her father was not so fine. He had decided she should be a doctor, but she had decided, after a brief study at the University of Zurich, that medicine was not her cup of tea. The only alternative her father saw for her was to get married. But marrying the man *he* had chosen was not to her liking either.

Going off to visit her uncle in Australia seemed like a good idea.

Her father, after much blustering, agreed—doubtless because he was at his wit's end. Here she was, an intelligent, attractive young woman, and, in his opinion, too independent for her own good. A short separation, he convinced himself, would tame her and return her to his household more willing to follow his suggestions.

Her seven younger sisters envied her. Her mother, teary at the parting, anxiously reminded her to care for her complexion and fitted her out with clothes that would not shame her in the eyes of their distant relatives.

But her uncle's family, though impressed, didn't envy this girl from Cracow her fine clothes. Who needed white gowns and high button shoes living in the outback?

What they did envy was her complexion. To the women of Victoria with their sun-scorched, windburned cheeks, the soft white skin of their city cousin seemed remarkable.

The secret? It was no secret at all, Helena Rubinstein informed them. It was just a "little pot of face cream."

Generously she shared the cream with her cousins, and, when her supply grew low, she wrote home for more. But, by that time, friends of her cousins also wanted the cream. Before she knew it, she was in business.

There was nothing about the young Helena Rubinstein that would indicate a great head for business—if you ignored the fact that she was better at keeping figures than her merchant father. He had always been more interested in reading books than in keeping them. Helena had often helped him keep his bookkeping in order. Working together, they often clashed.

Impulsively, when she was fourteen years old, with her parents away for a few days, she sold all the heavy, old furniture in her bedroom to a secondhand dealer. With the money she bought light, attractive new pieces.

Her father was enraged. Those old pieces were antiques, he told her, priceless in his estimation. He immediately went out and bought back every piece she had sold. Without another word, he returned to the store all her new things, restoring her room to its plain and stuffy look.

Though angry at the time, it was a lesson that must have burned itself into Helena's mind. Her own buying of antiques, many years later, filled five different houses in five different countries. Money spent on antiques was money well spent, she believed. That may have been part of her father's contribution to her future life.

But her mother's contribution was perhaps even more important. Into her daughter's luggage, when Helena left for the visit to her uncle in Australia, she tucked twelve little pots of face cream.

"I often find it hard to believe that my own business, which has introduced more than a thousand beauty preparations, started with a single face cream used every night by my mother."

Though Mrs. Rubinstein was rather old fashioned ("makeup" was unknown outside of the theater in those days), she would dab a little cream onto her daughters' cheeks whenever they had been out in the wind or the snow.

The cream was pretty much a homemade concoction put together by a family doctor for a small circle of Cracow patients. Though it was made of nothing more than wax, mineral oil, and sesame, Helena liked to say, "It's made of a wonderful mixture of rare herbs, the essence of Oriental almonds, extracts from the bark of an evergreen tree. . . .

"Certainly she wanted to pass on other, greater gifts to her daughter than just good skin care," Helena noted of her mother. "But what parent can tell when some such fragmentary gift of knowledge or wisdom will enrich her children's lives? Or how a small seed of information passed from one generation to another may generate a new science, a new industry—a seed which neither the giver nor the receiver can truly evaluate at the time."

When her uncle refused to see any lasting value in the new business of beauty she was creating, Helena moved to Melbourne. With a loan from a friend she had met on shipboard en route to Australia, she rented a little shop, painted it white, used the skirts of her fashionable dresses to make draperies for the windows, put in wicker and rattan furniture (the cheapest thing she could find), and started the first cosmetic industry in the world.

"The women streamed in," she related in her autobiography, "mostly out of curiosity since a beauty salon was unheard of in those days. I saw to it that they stayed on for advice. Few left without a jar of my hand-labeled cream. . . .

"Sydney's foremost woman journalist, who had heard of Australia's first beauty salon, came and interviewed me. She reported every word I said in her widely read column, adding that my Valaze cream (the name she gave to the doctor's concoction) was the answer to every Australian woman's prayer. I was deluged with letters and money orders from every part of the country. I was overwhelmed. I didn't have the stock to fill the demand!"

She wrote and acknowledged every order by hand, sitting up

nights to do so, and offered to return the money for the orders she couldn't fill at the moment. "Only one person asked for her money back!" she said.

Helena began to note that the women who came into her shop for the cream had different skin textures. She realized "that wonderful as my cream was . . . it could not solve every irregularity. I would have to learn how to create new creams and lotions to suit different skin types. I began to classify these as oily, dry, combination, and normal."

Suddenly she saw that four skin-types would require four different products and that the four products would have to be expanded into four related lines catering to each skin-type. She would need, she figured, a cream, a lotion, a soap, and other preparations for all these differently textured skins. The young Helena Rubinstein caught a sudden glimpse into her future. The beauty horizon stretched infinitely onward.

She summoned the Polish doctor named Lykusky to Australia where he could concoct the creams under her direction. She also sent for two of her sisters to help with her expanding business. Beside selling the cream, she took it upon herself to instruct women individually on the art of proper skin care, something no one had ever done as a business before. Loving every minute of it, Helena worked eighteen hours a day, a pattern she followed almost every day for the rest of her life.

When she was not working in the shop or checking over her accounts, she studied every available medical and pharmaceutical book on skin care. She came to think of her kitchen as her laboratory.

Marriage to Edward Titus, a young American newspaperman, in 1908 and the birth of two sons, Roy and Horace, didn't lessen her passion for her work.

The new business of beauty spawned competitors all over the world. Some unashamedly marked up the price of their products 900 percent. Excited rather than discouraged by competition, Rubinstein steadfastly refused to raise her prices above the middle range. "My conscience wouldn't permit it," she said.

No other creator of beauty products (not even her closest competitor, Elizabeth Arden) brought forth the kind of homage Helena Rubinstein received. She was "Madame" to everybody.

"If there's anything Madame likes as much as work," a friend said, "it's people with problems. She loves to give advice, money, and presents—in that order."

Helping others, giving presents, and working filled Helena Rubinstein's life. She drew into her company five of her sisters, an uncounted number of nieces and nephews, and, later, her son Roy.

But, although her business flourished, her twenty-five-year marriage didn't. Her husband disapproved of her always being away from home. "But I was so completely caught up in the web of my work and planning that I considered the business my first duty. I realize what a failure I must have been at that time as a wife, even as a mother," she said when her marriage ended. "I had no one to blame but myself."

A year after her divorce, Helena Rubinstein married a Russian prince, a recent American citizen, who, according to *Life* magazine, "regards his strong-willed wife with a combination of amazed admiration and amused affection."

Her second marriage inspired Rubinstein to establish a male cosmetic line bearing the prince's name. It occurred to her then that, by concentration on women alone, she had tapped only one-half of the beauty market business. "Men could be a lot more beautiful," she observed, with the sense of excitement that the glimpse of any new horizon always gave her.

Helena Rubinstein not only founded the first beauty business but was the lifetime proprietor of one of the world's most famous cosmetic enterprises.

Her worldwide operations sold 423 different products in one hundred countries. She employed thirty thousand people in factories, laboratories, and salons in fourteen countries.

In New York she lived in a twenty-six-room penthouse, filled with original art works by Picasso, Dufy, Chagall, Miro, and other famous painters.

She loved to wear great masses of jewelry (some once owned by Catherine of Russia), which she casually kept in a cardboard box beneath her bed. Yet she carried her lunch in a brown paper bag and practiced small economies in her households.

It wasn't unusual for her to go about her apartment turning out the lights in the interest of economy. Once, when an employee let the elevator in her Paris penthouse get away, going unoccupied all the way to the bottom, she scolded, "Do you realize how much it costs to make that go up and down?"

"I am a practical person," she once said. "I hate waste."

But, like many Jews whose roots were dug into the soil of *tze-*

dakah, Rubinstein did not count "giving" as a waste. She gave generously to philanthropic causes all over the world. In 1953, when she was eighty-two years old, she created the Helena Rubinstein Foundation to give funds to organizations concerned with health, medical research, and rehabilitation.

"My fortune comes from women and should benefit them and their children to better their quality of life."

Long before the start of the women's liberation movement, she was convinced that education for women was vital. She made scholarship grants to encourage young women to go to college and to get into nontraditional careers. Feeling strongly Jewish, she was particularly generous in her gifts to Israel. She founded the Helena Rubinstein Pavilion of Contemporary Art in Tel Aviv. Among her many contributions was her support of the America-Israel Cultural Foundation, and she sponsored countless scholarships for young Israelis.

When she died in 1965 at the age of ninety-four, her foundation carried on her gift-giving. A three-million-dollar grant (the foundation's largest gift) was given in 1987 for the United States Holocaust Memorial Museum in Washington, D.C. Facing the Jefferson Memorial, the museum will document the history of the Holocaust to teach future generations its tragic lessons. Funds will be used for a Helena Rubinstein Cinema /Lecture Hall in the Cultural and Conference Center.

Portraits of this princess of the beauty business were painted by seventeen noted artists. (Picasso had sketched her many times but never finished a portrait.) All showed the stern, square lines of a serious face, hair pulled back from a high forehead, in a fashion that was hers alone. ("I'm too busy to bother with it.") And, though each showed a different vision of this one woman, one quality dominated in all. A magazine writer called it "integrity."

She was, as another described her, using a more biblical term, a "matriarch . . . Jewish mother and ruler of the tribe."

18
RUTH WESTHEIMER

"The more people are educated, the more they want to be sexually literate, too."

Ruth Westheimer (1929–   ), psychotherapist, sex education pioneer.

*There are shows educating
people in furniture
upholstering, plant care,
and cooking—why not
sex? said Dr. Ruth.*

A small, middle-aged woman hailed a cab and asked to be taken to 30 Rockefeller Plaza. At the sound of her voice with its heavy German accent, the cabdriver turned to look at her. "Dr. Ruth?"

No, the New York taxi driver wasn't a long-lost relative. He had never seen this woman before. But he had heard her—on a Sunday night radio call-in show.

Once you hear Dr. Ruth, you are not likely to forget her. And it's not only because she has an accent and rolls her r's, it's because she talks about sex. That's right, S-E-X.

Not what you shouldn't do—but what you should do and how to go about it. And, most of all, how to enjoy it.

When she began her fifteen-minute radio show in 1980 (later to become a full hour), it was the first time in the history of talk shows that anything so personal was discussed over the air. It was the first time too that the enjoyment of sex was talked about as if it could be learned just as easily as any other human activity.

"So why not?" asked Ruth Westheimer. The words came out sounding more like "So vy not?"

"There are shows educating people in furniture upholstering, plant care, and cooking," she said. "Vy not sex?" And, though she was perfectly serious, an impish giggle escaped as she said, "Vy not share a few recipes on the air?"

Dr. Ruth not only shared a few recipes but she answered whatever questions about sex were called in to her, and her answers were always warm, frank, and often funny.

A tiny woman with eyes that squinched almost closed when she smiled (and she seemed to be smiling all the time), Dr. Ruth handed out sex tips the way doting aunts hand out cookies.

Only 4' 7" tall, her feet dangled above the floor when she sat on an ordinary chair. In restaurants she often sat on a telephone book. Her voice occasionally squeaked like a screen door, and her laugh often trilled into a tee-hee-hee.

The fact that she was raising eyebrows—not to mention gasps and snickers—by doing what no one had ever dared to do over the air before bothered her not at all.

"I am promoting sexual literacy in a time of unprecedented sexual freedom," Dr. Ruth insisted.

Like the pioneers in sex research education (Kinsey, Masters and Johnson, Helen Singer Kaplan, Mary Calderone), Ruth West-heimer believed, "The more people are educated, the more they want to be sexually literate, too."

But being sexually literate was not something Dr. Ruth talked about with cover-up words and solemn manner. She talked exactly to the point and plainly. The woman Americans were listening to talked just as plainly as if she were talking about cabbages and cucumbers. She said vagina when she meant vagina and penis when she meant penis.

"Holding back from sexual pleasure does not make you good," is one of the things Dr. Ruth told her listeners with marriage bed problems.

She was backed up, not only by her own Orthodox Jewish back-ground, but by solid Jewish wisdom that has come down through the ages. According to talmudic belief, having sex without pleasure makes you not a saint but a sinner.

The Jewish tradition, she'll tell you, actually has quite a lot to say about sex. "Most of it, remarkably in keeping with today's thinking."

Quoting from a passage in the Mishnah (compilation of Jewish laws and learning), Dr. Ruth said that it's the husband's obligation to provide, not only food and shelter for his wife, but also sexual satisfaction. "The Talmud," she added, "occasionally gets quite poetic on the subject." In Judaism, there is no shame in the body.

In Judaism, as well, there is no ban on humor. As the Talmud says: "A lesson taught with humor is a lesson well retained."

Her advice covered almost anything you can imagine having to do with the enjoyment of sex—including contraceptives and "safer sex." "I never talk about 'safe sex' because I don't know if there's such a thing."

On a typical broadcast she told kids not to rush their first sexual experiences. But she gave them sound, practical advice for the first time—after they decided they were ready.

To an eighteen-year-old whose boy friend of a month was urging intercourse, Dr. Ruth gave this advice:

"Don't do it. You know why I'm saying that? Because one month is a very short time. Also, because I hear in your question that he is putting pressure on you. Listen to that inner voice that says you would like to wait. Tell him that Dr. Westheimer told you that you can hug and kiss and neck and pet, but that you are just not ready."

"Wait until I'm ready," the caller echoed.

"Absolutely," Dr. Ruth said, "and then only with a good contraceptive."

Years of working with pregnant teenagers at Planned Parenthood, Dr. Ruth said, made her a fanatic about contraception. Almost everyone who called in, no matter what the age or what the problem, was asked: "Do you have good contraception?" If the answer was hesitant, she told the caller where to go for help.

From the day her voice first went out over the air, it was clear that there were a lot of young people who wanted to know a lot of things that their parents, teachers, doctors, ministers, rabbis, and even books had never told them.

Hundreds of callers flooded the station every time Dr. Ruth was on. No question was a foolish one to her.

"Look, I understand," Dr. Ruth said with warm respect to one caller. And she did. Because, magically, she answered the unspoken question the caller really wanted to ask.

Shortly after she began her talk show, Dr. Ruth herself was deluged with requests to appear on other talk shows. "I was on a half dozen local New York programs," she said happily. Yet her frank speech sometimes embarrassed her talk-show hosts. Quite a few people gasped in disapproval at her easy way of talking about what ordinarily no one ever talked about.

The *New York Times*, the *International Herald Tribune*, the London *Times*, the *Wall Street Journal* all ran interviews with her. She was asked by several publishers, "Are you interested in writing a book?" She was, already having two in mind.

"In less than a year I had gone from being an obscure, unemployed college professor to a national celebrity."

Ruth Westheimer believed in the worth of what she was doing. So did her husband, Fred, a telecommunications engineer, and their two children, Miriam (Dr. Ruth's daughter from an earlier marriage) and their son, Joel.

She believed in it so much that she was quite willing to communicate sexual literacy through almost every possible way: four books, a syndicated column, radio and television programs, a board game, a home video, TV commercials, T-shirts, and university lectures.

Being a celebrity was something new to her.

"Who would have thought that I'd be going to Saks to have my hair done? Who would have thought that I'd ever get $55,000 for a book contract? When I came to this country, I was earning seventy-five cents an hour as a cleaning woman."

In 1939, when Karola Ruth Siegel was ten years old, she was sent off to a school in Switzerland. It was very early in the morning, barely light, when she said goodbye to her mother and grandmother at the Frankfurt, Germany, railroad station.

"It was drizzling and gray. The train made a lot of noise, the big steam engines hissing and bellowing."

She pressed her face against the train window and saw her mother and grandmother running after the slowly moving train, waving a last goodbye.

She never again returned to her home in Frankfurt, Germany— or ever again saw either of her parents or her grandparents.

Six months after she left her home, Karola was an orphan. It was supposed that her family died in Auschwitz. She didn't know. There were no records.

The one hundred German Jewish children in the Swiss school, all orphaned in the Holocaust, were considered charity cases. The boys' schooling was continued, but the girls were taught only to be maids. It became the duty of the Jewish orphans to act as servants to the Swiss children.

My day during the school year (Karola Ruth wrote in her diary):

> I get up at six-thirty in the morning. I get dressed. We wake up the children at seven. . . .
>
> Then came a list of the chores required of her: helping the children dress, setting tables, cleaning, putting the children to bed for a nap, sweeping, bathing the children, mending, and putting the children to bed.
>
> . . . and at seven-thirty I too go to bed.

My day during vacation:

> At six-fifteen Hannelore comes to wake us up. . . . First we line up the benches in the dining room, then we go

to the dormitories and help make the beds. When we're through with this, we go to the washrooms and help to comb the children's hair. Then we have coffee. After I've had my coffee I get a pail of water from the kitchen and a broom and sweep the floors of the hallways and the toilets. Then I wipe everything on the outside, and then I clean the toilets. When all this is done, I mop the floor with a wet mop. . . . When I'm through with my chores, I join Hannelore upstairs and together we do the bedrooms. By then it's eleven-thirty and time to eat.

It was the story of Sarah Carew in *The Little Princess* by Frances Hodgson Burnett all over again—only one hundred times magnified. In the story, Sarah was saved by a pet monkey and a kind gentleman. In Karola's school, each orphaned student had to find his or her own salvation. And, like the character in the story, Karola Ruth set about to find hers.

"I only realized it much later, but my father gave me a wonderful gift: a love of and joy in learning. At the time, I didn't understand how unusual it was that he would take me, a girl, to synagogue and spend so much time teaching me things. In the Orthodox Jewish culture, this is how you normally behaved toward a boy, so maybe my father knew I was the only child he would have, that I would have to serve as both boy and girl."

Her yearning to know about things sometimes got her into trouble with the house matron. Once she was punished for knocking on a window of a boy's dorm room. But that didn't deter her from continuing to negotiate with the boys to lend her their books.

She had always loved reading. She had even loved reading books she could barely understand, like the ones kept locked in a high cabinet in her Orthodox Jewish home in Frankfurt. She had tried to read them anyway, in secret, climbing on a chair to reach the cabinet key and replacing the key after she put the book back. One of them was a copy of a marriage manual written by a Dutch gynecologist.

What she had read there came in handy in the school. It was Karola Ruth who told the other girls that leaving a window open wasn't the way babies were born or that setting a sugar lump on the sill for the stork didn't insure that the new baby would be a boy.

"It's very hard for me to write or even to talk about these years," said Dr. Ruth in her autobiography, *All in a Lifetime*. "In all the hundreds of interviews I've given since I've been Dr. Ruth, I've never really discussed them. It's mostly because of the message that was so successfully drummed into our heads during those six years in Switzerland: Never complain. You're lucky to be alive."

Even later when her own children asked her what it was like to be ten years old, without a mother or father, she couldn't talk about it. "I changed the subject," she said.

Karola Ruth was sixteen when she left Switzerland. In Israel she dropped her German name, Karola, and took her biblical middle name, Ruth. She had no high school diploma, and her occupation was maid. She worked first on a kibbutz and then went to Jerusalem to study to qualify as a kindergarten teacher.

She joined the Hagganah (the underground group fighting for Israeli statehood and independence from the British, who still governed Palestine). She learned to assemble a Sten gun with her eyes closed. She could fire five bullets into what she called "the red thing in the middle of the target."

In 1949, on Ruth's twentieth birthday, the warning for a mortar attack sounded. But she didn't want to go into the shelter without a book and was caught in the firing. Shrapnel tore into both of her ankles, and it was long weeks of skillful care in the hospital that saved both feet from amputation.

One year later, she and her husband, a fellow student, left Jerusalem for Paris so he could study medicine. It was after a second marriage (which also lasted a short time and ended in a friendly manner) that Ruth came to live in America.

Three years later she got her master's degree in sociology from the New School in New York City.

It was working with Planned Parenthood that led Ruth into becoming a psychosexual therapist. If she was going to continue talking to people about sex, she decided, she had to learn more about it.

"People would ask me questions about sex, and I realized I didn't know enough to answer."

So she went into training as a therapist at New York Hospital-Community Medical Center. Then she earned her doctorate in the Interdisciplinary Study of the Family at Columbia University and became an adjunct associate professor at New York University.

When this little woman with a German accent came to the United States in 1956, she had certificates only as a kindergarten teacher and a housemaid. Thirty years later, the German Jewish girl who began life as Karola Ruth Siegel was one of eighty-seven prominent people honored during the Statue of Liberty 100th birthday celebration in 1986. All were American citizens born in other countries.

"If anyone would have told me," she told journalists, "that I'd be known across the United States as Dr. Ruth, I would have said that they were joking."

19

ROSALYN
YALOW

"My specialty is thinking. I think it's
the greatest fun in the world to take
a problem and analyze it."

Rosalyn Yalow (1921–   ), medical physicist.

*The discovery was like
identifying a teaspoon of
sugar in a lake 62 miles
long, 62 miles wide, and
30 feet deep.*

Bustling about her Bronx kosher kitchen, Rosalyn Yalow was everybody's picture of an ordinary Jewish housewife.

The small, brick Tudor-style house in which she and her husband Aaron, a physics professor at Manhattan's Cooper Union, lived for thirty years and brought up two children was a Jewish house. You could tell by the *mezuzah* on the doorframe and the separate Passover dishes stored in the attic.

But there was nothing ordinary about Rosalyn Yalow.

She was the professional star in the family. Rosalyn Yalow was the second woman ever to win the Nobel Prize in physiology or medicine.

"You keep kosher?" people sometimes asked her in amazement.

Her answer was always with a shrug. "So how much more work is it to have a kosher home?"

Rosalyn Yalow would probably be the last person on earth to look upon herself as extraordinary. She saw her remarkable accomplishments very simply.

"I did what I wanted to do," she said.

Rosalyn grew up in the Bronx. Her parents, Simon and Clara Sussman, were Jewish immigrants.

Her family liked to tell how her older brother, Alexander, wacked with a ruler across the knuckles by a strict teacher on his first day of school, came home crying. Five years later, on her first day of school, Rosalyn was similarly whacked, but she grabbed the ruler and hit back.

Her husband admired this quality in her long before they were married; her medical partner valued it.

Other scientists in the field of physics were not always as accepting. Some were downright antagonistic. Their reasons: she was a woman; she was Jewish; she was aggressive.

Her children grew up with it.

Said her daughter Elanna, "My mother wasn't really that different from other people's mothers, in terms of making us eat and yelling at us if we didn't."

But she was different in other respects.

She graduated from Hunter College in Manhattan at nineteen, magna cum laude, and Phi Beta Kappa, having been elected as a junior. Even so, her future didn't look very bright. It was the time of the Great Depression and jobs were scarce. When she applied to Purdue for a graduate assistantship in physics, the school wrote back to her professor: "She's a Jew and a woman, and we can never get her a job afterward."

Meanwhile she took shorthand and got a job as secretary to a Columbia University biochemist. When the University of Illinois offered her a teaching assistantship in 1941, Yalow firmly tore up all her steno notebooks. She was the first woman admitted to that program since 1917.

She earned her Ph.D. degree in physics in January 1945, already married to a fellow physics student named A. Aaron Yalow, son of a rabbi from Upstate New York. Later she became the mother of Benjamin and Elanna.

Elanna, at that time in junior high school, said, "She'd come home at 5:45 with packages from the supermarket. She'd prepare dinner and by 7:30 P.M. she'd almost always go back to work."

Her work was in her nearby lab at the Veterans Administration Medical Center in New York City's borough of the Bronx.

"My specialty is thinking," Yalow said. "I think it's the greatest fun in the world to take a problem and analyze it."

Her son, Benjamin, saw part of his mother's will to succeed as "a passion for order and clarity. When a problem comes up, it's that it must be solved. She would," he suggested with a small smile, "make a perfectly acceptable hero."

"A hero, me?" she probably would have said at that, pushing her dark, wavy hair off her face.

"I'm a very ordinary person who's been very lucky" was the way she described herself.

She was "lucky," she said, that she married a man who accepted her aspirations, encouraged her, and didn't complain when she threw a few things into an overnight bag and flew down to Washington, D.C., to advise the government on nuclear radiation; or flew up to Dartmouth to teach the tricks of radioimmunoassay; or spent half the night in the lab, learning more about the chemistry of the body.

Lucky, she thought, that she chose nuclear medicine at a time when the field was new and almost untouched.

Lucky too in her choice of the physician Sol Berson as a partner.

She was lucky, she said, that she and Berson worked so well together. They sat at facing desks and bounced ideas back and forth until neither could remember whose idea it first was. They could both become terribly excited about seemingly impossible possibilities.

"They would come into a room," a colleague said, "and argue and bounce things off each other and throw ideas around. Then they'd go running out to the lab to test whatever it was, wildly flying around." Said another colleague, they went "day and night at ninety miles an hour."

"We've always been free from the prejudices of the rest of the field," Yalow said. Unafraid, she meant, to come into conflict with the conventional medical wisdom of the time.

Jews, by the very nature of their Jewishness, she pointed out, lack blind respect for voices of authority.

"I'm very disciplined. I've always put my eye on where I'm going. Trivial things don't matter to me, and I'm willing to make compromises, except in principle."

"Principle" was something very important to Rosalyn Yalow. And it had nothing to do with luck.

For instance, on principle, the partners did not patent their discovery of radioimmunoassay (RIA).

It was research in diabetes that led them to invent a technique that won Yalow the Nobel Prize five years after Berson's death.

RIA used radioactivity to permit measurement of infinitesimal traces of substances in blood or tissues. With it they were able to measure a substance never before measurable because it was so small, the body's own circulating insulin.

According to the Nobel Committee: "To find it was like identifying a teaspoon of sugar in a lake 62 miles long, 62 miles wide, and 30 feet deep. To measure it was like measuring a sugar cube dissolved in Lake Erie."

Since its development in 1959, RIA has become almost as useful as the microscope in medical laboratories. Yalow and Berson went on to develop similar procedures for measuring other hormones in body tissues. Today there are RIAs for hundreds of hormones, viruses, drugs, and other substances of biologic interest.

In 1978 the total profits from RIA procedures ran into the tens of millions of dollars. They provided a $300-million-a-year market for the companies producing them—but no money profit for Berson or Yalow.

Said Dr. Yalow: "In my day scientists did not always think of things as being patentable. We made a scientific discovery. Once it was published, it was open to the world."

It was a matter of principle.

It was a matter of principle, too, in the way Yalow gave a party. The year before she won the Nobel Prize, she became the first woman to win the Albert Lasker Basic Medical Research Award. To celebrate, she decided to throw a party for her staff.

"I got a $10,000 award," she told her secretary. "Let's have it catered." But, for a woman who enjoyed making matzah balls and turkey stuffing for holidays, having a party catered wasn't exactly like making a party herself. "I ended up cooking four turkeys at home, and I made potato salad here in the lab."

Perhaps that's why her staff saw this Jewish housewife from the Bronx less as an aggressive scientist than as a sort of "earth mother." It never surprised them when she brought cookies to their weekly meetings and kept reminding them to wear their galoshes on the way home.

At 6:30 on the morning of October 13, 1977, Rosalyn Yalow—physicist, wife, and mother—was sitting at her desk at the VA when the famous call came from Stockholm. A call from her husband followed and ended with "You'd better go home and change your clothes." She rushed home, changed, and was back in her lab well before the press and TV cameras descended upon her.

She was the sixth woman ever to win a Nobel science award, the second in medicine, the first to be wholly American-educated—and the only woman scientist who was both a Nobelist and a Jewish housewife.

20

ALBERT EINSTEIN

"The pursuit of knowledge for its own sake, an almost fanatical love of justice, and the desire for personal independence—these are the features of the Jewish tradition which make me thank my stars that I belong to it."

Albert Einstein (1879–1955), theoretical and mathematical physicist.

He changed
the world.

On August 2, 1939, Albert Einstein, one of the greatest scientists who ever lived, was writing a letter to the president of the United States.

He worked at it, sitting in his small study, writing on a pad on his knee. Every so often, he rose to pace the room in thought. His wildly waving white hair made a halo around his head. The bedroom slippers on his feet—he wore them constantly in the house and sometimes even out on the street—softly slip-slopped with each step.

Occasionally he stopped to gaze out the window onto the narrow street shaded by tall oak and elm trees. Then he seated himself again to continue with the letter. When it was completed, he reread it carefully.

It was addressed to President Franklin D. Roosevelt, and it said something so fantastic that, written by anyone else, it would not have been believed.

Because of recent discoveries, Einstein wrote, it was likely that the energy in the atom could be released explosively. This meant, he said, that a bomb could be made that would be greater and more destructive than anything yet imagined. It must be feared, the letter pointed out, that the Germans would try to make such a bomb.

The letter did not have to say what would happen if they did. World War II had been launched by the Nazis. If Hitlerism spread over the world, not only all Jews but all thinking people everywhere would be destroyed.

Einstein's deep-set, dark eyes under bushy brows remained fixed for a long time on the letter in his hands.

Writing this letter was a matter of great inner turmoil for him. He was a humanitarian Jew, a lover of peace and truth, an absolute pacifist. He regarded life as sacred. "It is the supreme value, to which all other values are subordinate," he had once said. At the age of twenty-six he had formulated the Theory of Relativity which

159

had helped to inaugurate the nuclear age. Now, at sixty, he was one of the few that saw his discovery could be used to threaten all humankind.

This man who had received the 1921 Nobel Prize in physics, and who had humbly given away the prize money to charity, had done more to revolutionize scientific thinking than any other individual. His name led the list of the famous who signed petitions protesting miscarriages of justice and advocating world disarmament. Yet he hesitated signing the letter he had just written, wondering if it should be sent off to the president or torn up.

His decision would be a fateful one.

What was as clear to him as it would be eventually to the president of the country was that the United States had to produce such a bomb before Germany did.

"If we are to resist the powers that threaten intellectual and individual freedom, we must be very conscious of the fact that freedom itself is at stake. . . ." The words were his own and he had said them in 1933, the same year Hitler had seized power in Germany.

On the quiet, tree-lined street below his window, in Princeton, New Jersey, Einstein saw the specter of armed Nazis as he had seen them roaming the streets of Germany.

He had come, a Jewish refugee from Nazi Germany, with his second wife, Elsa, to live in the United States and continue with his research at the Princeton Institute for Advanced Studies.

Though he didn't know it, he was the most famous citizen in the town. His neighbors would often rush to the windows to see him, dressed in baggy pants and a sweater, walking down the street in his bedroom slippers. Without Elsa around to remind him—she had died in 1936—Einstein often forgot to change into his shoes. A crowd often gathered at the door of a Princeton drug store to look in at the famous man standing at the counter, licking an ice cream cone.

He loved Princeton. He loved living in his modest two-story, gray frame house. He loved the freedom of inquiry that inspired Americans. "As long as I have any choice, I will stay only in a country where political liberty, toleration, and the equality of all citizens before the law is the rule," he said when he became an American citizen.

For Einstein the key to the future of the world lay in the minds of men. Without freedom of thought, no scientific progress would be possible.

Freedom.

Albert Einstein turned away from his window, picked up his pen, and signed the letter.

That letter is now famous. It helped to launch the American effort that resulted in production of the nuclear reactor and the fission bomb that defeated Japan, Hitler's ally, and ended the war.

Albert Einstein had an abiding passion for freedom. As a child, he had hated playing "soldiers." He hated the regimented system of his German school: the rote learning and the constant drill. He hated having to memorize a given answer to every question. Reciting in class was to him like marching in mindless unison to the empty beat of a drum.

He preferred to stare into space and wonder about the world around him. ("The great ocean of truth lay all undiscovered before me," he wrote some time later.) It was not in his school books he learned that "the most incomprehensible thing about the world is that it is comprehensible."

In the Munich school he attended until he was fifteen, young Einstein was always in trouble. His mind wandered; his memory, never very dependable in ordinary matters, often failed him. (Years later, it astounded many that this man with the great scientific intellect never could remember how many honorary degrees he received or to how many learned societies he belonged.)

For a while, when he was a child, his parents feared that he might be retarded, for he didn't speak at all until he was several years old and didn't speak fluently even at the age of nine. After saying something, he would repeat his own words softly, a habit which stayed with him all his life.

When his father, Hermann Einstein, asked his son's headmaster what profession the boy should adopt, the answer, in slightly different words, was "What does it matter? He'll never make a success of anything."

Einstein's curiosity about science first came, not at school, but at home. When he was four or five years old his father showed him a compass. The jumping needle enchanted him. What was the mysterious attraction that always made it point north?

"Something deeply hidden has to be behind things," was the thought that remained with him.

Einstein looked on music as he looked on science—with a sense of wonder and excitement. He had started taking violin lessons when he was six years old. "I really began to learn only when I was about thirteen," he said, "mainly after I had fallen in love with Mozart's sonatas." Mozart was his ideal. In Mozart's music he found "a purity and a simplicity" that seemed not composed but part of the universe.

Though he played both the violin and the piano, Einstein didn't consider himself musically talented. Neither did he feel especially gifted in other fields.

"I have no particular talent," he once said. "I am merely extremely inquisitive."

Stirring tea, he wondered why the tea leaves congregated at the center and not around the bottom of the cup. Walking on sand, he wondered why damp sand gave firm footing while dry sand or sand under water did not. He didn't stop thinking about such questions until he found a scientific explanation.

When Einstein was sixteen, attending school in Switzerland, he wondered what a wave of light would look like to someone keeping pace with it. At that time no one in the world could have given him a satisfactory answer.

He kept thinking about it. He constantly thought about it while he was finishing his education in Switzerland and while he was studying physics and mathematics for his degree in Zurich. He found the answer, finally—though it took him ten years. In the question was the germ of the Theory of Relativity.

He was twenty-six years old, an examiner in the Swiss Patent Office at Berne, the only job he had been able to find, when he worked it out. He was married and had two sons. He didn't have a laboratory to work in or a telescope or other instruments. All Einstein had was his head, a pen, and a pad of paper. It didn't occur to him that his jottings would result in the most extraordinary achievement of any human mind.

His Theory of Relativity was the last of four original papers he had finished in 1905. He had been scribbling at them for seven years, during spare moments at his work, on evenings, and on Sundays.

In the first, he described a method for measuring molecules.

In the second, he explained the photoelectric effect. This was the principle underlying the photo tube which made possible the worldwide communications of the twentieth century: the long distance telephone, talking motion pictures, radio, television, and the electron microscope. In the third, he presented a kinetic theory of heat.

And, in the fourth, by one equation, Einstein changed the way people looked at and thought about the world and everything in it. It was $E = MC^2$, energy is equal to mass multiplied by the square root of the velocity of light. To the dimensions of length, breadth, and width, he had added a fourth—motion or time-space.

For a long while, until his theory was proved during the solar eclipse of 1919, hardly anybody knew what Einstein was talking about. Even then, while many knew that he had discovered something, few knew exactly what it was. In the ten years following the sensational proof in 1919, more than five thousand books, in dozens of languages, were published to explain what Einstein called "Relativity," the relatedness of all things.

Einstein himself (who often wrote amusing bits of rhyming doggerel and liked to tell jokes) explained the theory very simply:

> When a nice girl sits on your lap for an hour, you think it's only a minute, but, when you sit on a hot stove for a minute, you think it's an hour—that's relativity.

In another story he explained how all things are related to each other:

> A thirsty, blind man is offered a drink of milk.
> "What is milk?" the blind man asked.
> He was told, "A white liquid."
> "Liquid I know, but what is white?"
> "White is like the feathers of a swan," was the answer.
> "Feathers I know, but what is a swan?" the blind man said.
> "A swan is a bird with a crooked neck."
> "Neck I know, but what is crooked?"
> To explain "crooked," his friend bent the blind man's arm.
> "Oh," said the blind man, nodding happily. "Now I know what milk is."

The world came to know Einstein, not only as a great thinker whose theories the average person could hardly hope to decipher, but also as an outstanding humane leader. When fame burst upon him, he used it as a way to further causes he believed in.

Like many Jewish families in Germany before the time of Hitler, Einstein's parents had felt more German than Jewish. The customs and traditions of the Jewish faith, his father had believed, were all part of "an ancient superstition."

With the beginnings of Nazi anti-Semitism, Albert Einstein became a Zionist. "I discovered for the first time that I was a Jew," he said. Zionism, the urge of people to return to their own land, reawakened the spirit of the scattered Jewish nation. It also reawakened Einstein to his own Jewishness.

He discovered in Judaism the humanism that was part of his own being. He discovered in himself a special reverence for a tradition that held in its essence that life is sacred.

Einstein once said, "The man who regards his own life and that of his fellow creatures as meaningless is not merely unhappy but hardly fit for life."

Einstein didn't feel that the world had developed by happenstance. He saw the hand of God in every law of the universe. Einstein believed that if only he knew what questions to ask nature, then the answers could be discovered.

"I want to know how God created this world," Albert Einstein said. "I want to know God's thoughts, the rest are details."

He kept searching for the single law that would explain the mysterious harmony of the universe. It was as intriguing to him when he was seventy as the mystery of the compass had been when he was only four. But the law of "Oneness" continued to elude him.

He liked to play with words: "Religion without science is blind, but science without religion is lame." Was there a truth in what he was saying? He thought so.

Einstein's irresistible longing to understand the secrets of nature did not interfere with his love for justice, nor did it keep him from trying to improve human conditions.

After the dropping of the atomic bomb helped to end World War II, Einstein worked to create a world government and a permanent end to war. He signed his name to a plea for the renunciation of nuclear weapons and the abolition of war.

Loudly, he spoke out against repression. Thinking people, he pointed out, must preserve freedom of expression.

With his help, the Hebrew University in Jerusalem was created. To raise money for Israel, he even appeared at a concert and played his violin.

After the death of the first president of Israel in 1952, Einstein was offered the presidency of the new state. He was surprised, humbly surprised. He didn't accept, but it was one of the high moments of his life, he said.

The scientist who changed the world's concept of the universe wrote these words: "The pursuit of knowledge for its own sake, an almost fanatical love of justice, and the desire for personal independence—these are the features of the Jewish tradition which make me thank my stars that I belong to it."

Notes and Sources

CHAPTER 1
Leo Baeck, *The Essence of Judaism* (1948).

Will Durant, *The Story of Philosophy* (1938).

H. M. Sachar, *The Course of Modern Jewish History* (1958).
  "Only to my Jewish nature," etc. (p. 398). Part of original quote
paraphrased. Original: "Because I was a Jew I found myself free
from prejudices which limited others in the use of their intellect,
and, being a Jew, I was prepared to enter opposition and to re-
nounce agreement with the 'compact majority.'"

Harry Gersh, *These Are My People* (1959).

Martin Buber, *Israel and the World* (1963).

Bernard Evslin, ed., *The Spirit of Jewish Thought* (1969).

Elie Wiesel, *One Generation After* (1970).

Raphael Patai, *The Jewish Mind* (1977).

Jacob S. Minkin, *The Shaping of the Modern Mind* (1963).

Chaim Raphael, *The Springs of Jewish Life* (1982).

CHAPTER 2
Marvin Lowenthal, "Theodor Herzl," *Molders of the Jewish Mind*
  (1916).

Theodor Herzl, "Experiences and Moods," an autobiographical
  sketch; "Diaries," translated, condensed, and annotated by Maurice Samuel; both in *Theodor Herzl, A Memorial*, edited by
  Meyer Weisgal (1929).

Abraham Leon Sachar, *A History of the Jews,* pp. 353–361 (1939).

Nathan Ausubel, *Pictorial History of the Jewish People,* pp. 300–306, 323 (1953).

H. M. Sachar, *The Course of Modern Jewish History,* pp. 269–283 (1958).

Amos Elon, *Herzl* (1975).

CHAPTER 3
Marie Syrkin, *Golda Meir: Woman with a Cause* (1963).

Golda Meir, autobiography, *My Life* (1975).

CHAPTER 4
Avital Shcharansky with Ilana Ben-Josef, *Next Year in Jerusalem.*

"The Refuseniks," *Keeping Posted,* Vol. XXIV, No. 3, Dec. 1978.

Martin Gilbert, *Shcharansky: Hero of Our Time* (1986).

"Shcharansky: A Latter-Day Job," *Time,* Feb. 17, 1986.

"The Other Shcharansky," *Newsweek,* Sept. 1, 1986.

"This Year in Jerusalem," *Time,* Feb. 24, 1986.

Aron Hirt-Manheimer, taped interview.

Tape of speech at UAHC Conference, 1987.

CHAPTER 5
"Mississippi—'Everybody's Scared,' " *Newsweek,* July 6, 1964.

"The Crime Called Conspiracy," *Time,* Dec. 11, 1964.

"Civil Rights," *Time,* July 3, 1964.

William Bradford Huie, *Three Lives for Mississippi* (1965).

Mrs. Robert Goodman, "My Son Didn't Die in Vain," *Good Housekeeping*, May 1965.

Jack Mendelsohn, *The Martyrs: Sixteen Who Gave Their Lives for Racial Justice* (1966).

CHAPTER 6
Betty Friedan, *The Feminine Mystique* (1963).

Paul Wilkes, "Mother Superior to Women's Lib," *New York Times Magazine*, Nov. 29, 1970.

Betty Friedan, *It Changed My Life: Writings on the Women's Movement* (1976).

Lynn Gilbert and Galen Moore, *Particular Passions* (1981).

Betty Friedan, *The Second Stage* (1981).

American Jewish Biographies (1982).

Marilyn French, "The Emancipation of Betty Friedan," *Esquire*, Dec. 1983.

Milton Meltzer, *Betty Friedan: A Voice for Women's Rights* (1985).

Interview, *Tikkun*, Jan./Feb. 1988.

CHAPTER 7
Current Biography, 1975.

Essie E. Lee, *Women in Congress* (1979).

Peggy Lamson, *In the Vanguard: Six American Women in Public Life* (1979).

Esther Steherman, *American Political Women* (1980).

American Jewish Biographies (1982).

Press clippings (*New York Times, New York Post, Gazette, Daily News, New York Newsday*), Nov. 1982-Oct. 1984.

"Biographical Highlights," Office of the District Attorney, Brooklyn, N.Y., 1986.

Isaiah Kuperstein, "A Race against Time: Amidst Controversy, the Justice Department Pursues Ex-Nazis," *Jewish Monthly*, Oct. 1987.

CHAPTER 8
Katherine Hinds, "Laura Geller '71: Wife, Mother, Rabbi."

Baccalaureate Address, 1971.

Laura Geller, packet of clippings of sermons, talks, articles from the Office of the Rabbi, Hillel Jewish Center, U.S.C., Los Angeles.

Laura Geller, "My Search for God," *Reform Judaism*, Winter 1987–88.

Laura Geller, "On Being a Jewish Feminist," 1982.

CHAPTER 9
About Lear, *New York Times Magazine*, June 24, 1973.

Current Biography, 1974.

Geoffrey Cowan, *See No Evil* (1979).

Geoffrey Wolff, "Shortcuts to the Heart," *Esquire*, Aug. 1981.

American Jewish Biographies (1982).

Horace Newcomb and Robert Alley, *The Producer's Medium* (1983).

CHAPTER 10
Frank Popper, *Origins and Development of Kinetic Art* (1968).

Aron Hirt-Manheimer, "A Conversation with Israeli Artist-Philosopher Yaacov Agam," *Reform Judaism*, Sept. 1981.

Yaacov Agam and Bernard Mendelbaum, *Art and Judaism* (1981).

"Tribute to Agam," *Congressional Record*, Senate, June 4, 1981.

Mira Avrech, Agam article, *People*, Apr. 20, 1981.

Current Biography Yearbook, 1981.

Frank Popper, *Agam*, Second Revised Edition (1983).

News release at dedication of Agam's Holy Ark and Eternal Light, *News*, Hebrew Union College, Oct. 25, 1987.

CHAPTER 11
Nat Hen, "Among the Wild Things," *New Yorker*, Jan. 22, 1966.

Current Biography, 1968.

Saul Braun, "Sendak Raises the Shade on Childhood," *New York Times Magazine*, June 7, 1970.

Something about the Author, Volume 27.

Books, *Time*, Dec. 10, 1973.

Roger Ricklefs, "Maurice Sendak's Pen Strips Children's Books of Their Innocence," *Wall Street Journal*, Thursday, Dec. 20, 1979.

Article, *New York Times Magazine*, Oct. 12, 1980.

Selma C. Lanes, *The Art of Maurice Sendak* (1980).

American Jewish Biographies (1982).

CHAPTER 12
Current Biography, 1969.

Isaac B. Singer, *Nobel Lecture* (1978).

David C. Gross, *Pride of Our People* (1979).

Paul Kewah, *Isaac Bashevis Singer: Story of a Storyteller* (1984).

CHAPTER 13
"Woody Allen: Rabbit Running," Cover story, *Time*, July 3, 1972.

Schickel, "Basic Allen," *New York Times Magazine*, Jan. 7, 1973.

Penelope Gill, "Guilty with an Explanation," Profile, *New Yorker*, Feb. 4, 1974.

Frank Rich, "Woody Allen Wipes the Smile off His Face," *Esquire*, May 1977.

Jack Kroll, "Woody, Funny But He's Serious," *Newsweek*, Apr. 24, 1978.

Natalie Gittelson, "The Maturing of Woody Allen," *New York Times Magazine*, Apr. 22, 1979.

Richard Grenier, "Woody Allen in the Limelight," *Commentary*, July 1979.

American Jewish Biographies (1982).

Richard Grenier, "Woody Allen on the American Character," *Commentary*, Nov. 1983.

Samuel Dresner, "Woody Allen Theologian?" *Midstream*, Mar. 1985.

Aryeh L. Gotlieb, "Troubled Jew," *Midstream*, Mar. 1985.

CHAPTER 14
Donald Zec and Anthony Fowles, *Barbra: A Biography of Barbra Streisand* (1981).

James Spada, *Streisand: The Woman and the Legend* (1981).

American Jewish Biographies (1982).

MJR, "Streisand's Tribute," *Near East Report*, Dec. 30, 1983.

Shaun Considine, *Barbra Streisand: The Woman, the Myth, the Music* (1985).

M. Z. Ribalow, "Barbra and Bashevis: A Different Yentl," *Midstream*, Mar. 1985.

CHAPTER 15
Music-Violinists, *Time*, Jan. 15, 1965.

Current Biography, 1975.

David Ewen, ed., *Musicians Since 1900: Performers in Concert and Opera* (1978).

Annalyn Swan, "Perlman, Prince of Fiddlers," *Readers Digest*, Aug. 1980.

Barbara Rowes, "Itzhak Perlman, Top Fiddle," *Newsweek*, Apr. 14, 1980.

Herbert Kupeferberg, "Itzhak Perlman—From a Long Line of Fiddlers," *Present Tense*, Winter 1981.

Itzhak Perlman, "Itzhak Perlman," *TV Guide*, Oct. 5–11, 1985.

Boris Schwarz, *Great Masters of the Violin* (1985).

Miriam Horn, "The Genius of Teaching Geniuses," conversation with Dorothy DeLay, *U.S. News & World Report*, July 27, 1987.

CHAPTER 16
"To Be Is to Do," *Ageing International,* information bulletin of
the International Federation on Ageing, Winter 1978.

Sharon Burde, "Jerusalem's Lifeline for the Old Fosters Aging
with Dignity," *St. Louis Jewish Light,* Jan. 2, 1980.

Danny Siegel, *Gym Shoes and Irises: Personalized Tzedakah* (1982).

Esther Hecht, "Where Age Is Not a Crime," *Jerusalem Post,* Nov.
13–19, 1983.

CHAPTER 17
Jo Swerling, "Beauty in Jars and Vials," Profile, *New Yorker,* June
30, 1928.

Current Biography, 1943.

Helena Rubinstein, autobiography, *My Life for Beauty* (1964).

Patrick O'Higgins, biography, *Madame* (1971).

T. F. James, "Princess of the Beauty Business," *Cosmopolitan,*
1971.

Maxine Fabe, biography for children, *Beauty Millionaire* (1972).

CHAPTER 18
Judy Bach, interview, *People,* Mar. 8, 1982.

Barbara Multer, biography, *The Dr. Ruth Phenomenon* (1987).

Don Carter, interview, *Seattle Post Intelligencer,* June 17, 1987.

William E. Geist, interview, *New York Times.*

Dr. Ruth Westheimer, autobiography, *All in a Lifetime* (1988).

Biographical notes from NBC.

Personal interview, Dec. 1987.

CHAPTER 19
Yalow's remarks, Jewish Academy of Arts and Sciences Dinner honoring Nobel Laureates, 1977.

Nobel Laureate speech, 1977.

Elizabeth Stone, "A Mme. Curie from the Bronx," *New York Times Magazine*, Apr. 9, 1978.

Article, *People*, Jan. 2, 1978.

Current Biography, 1978.

American Jewish Biographies (1982).

Dennis Overbye, "Lady Laureate of the Bronx," *Discover* magazine, June 1982.

Telephone interview, Aug. 1987.

CHAPTER 20
Current Biography, 1941.

Current Biography, 1953.

H. M. Sachar, *The Course of Modern Jewish History* (1958).

International Biographical Directory.

Henry Enoch Kagan, *Six Who Changed the World* (1963).

Ronald W. Clark, biography, *Einstein: The Life and Times* (1971).

David C. Gross, *Pride of Our People* (1979).

ADDITIONAL SOURCES
Goldberg, M. Hirsh. *The Jewish Connection.* Briarcliff Manor, New York: Stein & Day, 1976.

Greenberg, Martin H. *The Jewish Lists*. New York: Schocken Books, 1979.

Gross, David C. *Pride of Our People: The Stories of One Hundred Outstanding Jewish Men and Women*. New York: Doubleday & Co., Inc., 1979.

American Jewish Biographies. New York: Lakeville Press, Inc., Facts on File, Inc., 1982.

Koppman, Lionel, and Postal, Bernard. *Guess Who's Jewish in American History*. New York: Shapolsky Publishers, Second Revised Edition, 1986.

Boxer, Tim. *The Jewish Celebrity Hall of Fame*. New York: Shapolsky Publishers, 1987.

Commire, Anne, ed. *Something about the Author*. Detroit, Michigan: Gale Research Co.

Encyclopedic Dictionary of Judaica.

Current Biography. Wilson.

Current Biography Yearbooks. Wilson.

International Biographical Directory.